THE AUTHOR

Donald William Cox is especially well prepared to write this book by his background in public education. He has been Associate Director of Research and Information Services for the Montgomery County (Pennsylvania) Schools and Director of the Priestley Science Center Project for the Philadelphia school system. He has also served as Professor of Education at New York University and the University of Florida. He is a graduate of Montclair State College in New Jersey and holds the Master of Arts and the Doctor of Education degrees from Columbia University.

Dr. Cox is currently serving as the Director of Communications for Opportunities Industrialization Centers of America, an innovative manpower training venture under the leadership of the Reverend Leon Sullivan.

He has written over a dozen books, including "Profiles of American Ecologists" and "Explorers of the Ocean Depths."

THE CITY AS A
SCHOOLHOUSE

THE CITY AS A
SCHOOLHOUSE

The Story of the Parkway Program

DONALD WILLIAM COX

Judson Press, Valley Forge

LD
7501
.P5
P34

THE CITY AS A SCHOOLHOUSE

Copyright © 1972

Judson Press, Valley Forge, Pa. 19481

Photos on pages 3-4, 12, 21, 32, 53, 55, 56, 59, 107, 122, 129, 145, 169, 176 are by Joe Nettis. Photos on pages 44, 45, 50, 63, 69, 88, 90, 102, 114 are by Eileen Ahrenholz. Photo on page 116 by Carlton Read.

International Standard Book No. 0-8170-0552-8
Library of Congress Catalog Card No. 79-181559

Printed in the U.S.A.

"If the nation is successfully to survive the seventies, it must shatter the myth that education comes packaged only within classroom walls."

John W. Macy, Jr.
President: Corporation for
Public Broadcasting
May 13, 1971

For:
Cliff: who dreamed it,
John: who brought it to life,
and
Len: who helped sustain it.

Acknowledgements

Readers' Note on Source Material: Most of the material for this volume was obtained by using primary sources rather than secondary documentation. Although there have been many newspaper and magazine articles written about the Parkway Program during the first three years of its life, only two books have appeared so far in public print with any reference to this fascinating new educational alternative. In the already classic volume, *Crisis in the Classroom* (Random House, 1970), which many critics believe is the best education volume written in the last quarter century, the author, Charles Silberman, devotes eight pages to this school without walls. John Bremer's and Michael von Moschzisker's paperback, *School Without Walls* (Holt, Rinehart & Winston, 1971), is the other.

Fortunately, the author of this book (the first hardcover volume devoted exclusively to the Parkway Program and its important offshoots) was able personally to interview all of the key figures in the birth and growth of the effort over a three-year span—from 1968 through 1971. To these people, he is deeply indebted for their giving valuable time to discuss the merits of the program in a realistic manner. Without their friendly cooperaton there would have been no book. In some cases, i.e., Dr. Bremer, several interviews were conducted during the research period that preceded the writing of this volume.

The personages interviewed were as follows: Dr. John Bremer and Dr. Leonard Finkelstein, the first two Directors of the Program; Cy Schwartz, Director of Community Gamma; Dr. Mark Shedd, Superintendent of Schools of the School District of Philadelphia; Clifford Brenner, the founder of the Parkway Program and Administrative Assistant to School Board President Dilworth; Dr. Paul Goodman, one of America's leading educational philosophers and critics; Dr. Peter Buttenwieser, Director of the Durham Learning Center; Robert Blackburn, Director of the Office of Intergroup Education, Philadelphia Schools; Dr. Bernard Kelner, Superintendent of District No. 6 of the Philadelphia Schools; Dr. Richard Snyder, the founder of Project Learn; Bernard Ivens, math teacher in Community Gamma; Lisa Strick, Director of Public Relations for the Parkway Program; and numerous other teachers, parents, and students who helped make the effort the success that it is today. Special thanks also go to my loyal typist Mary Anne Twyman, who labored patiently over this manuscript.

DWC
Philadelphia, Pa.
September, 1971

Contents

PART I
THE MAKING OF
THE PARKWAY
PROGRAM

Introduction

"Our present system of public education, coercive in its methods, is a symptom and a major cause of our unsatisfactory way of life," said Ewald B. Nyquist, the New York State Commissioner of Education, recently. The crisis in our schools is a reflection of the larger crisis in our society as a whole and is a crisis whose resolution is not clear at this writing.

Most of today's public and private elementary and secondary schools of America are killers of our children's dreams through their systematic and oppressive mutilation of their minds. Several recent educational critics, such as Jonathan Kozol, Paul Goodman, Ronald Gross, John Holt, Charles Silberman, Neil Postman, and George Dennison, have documented in published works how our schools are educating children for docility instead of creative living. Students and teachers are both involved in a struggle to survive.

These grim, dull, joyless places, with their sterile atmospheres, have caused some parents and school administrators to seek meaningful alternatives so that we can reorganize our schools. They have been supported by these aforementioned educational critics who have each made a cry for some sort of reform before it is too late.

Crisis in the Classroom by Charles Silberman is probably the best of these reform-oriented books. In his monumental three-year study for the Carnegie Corporation, which originally was intended only as an in-depth analysis and critique of the shortcomings of teacher education in America, Silberman soon broadened his vision to include the actual arena of teaching—the schools themselves. In this hard-hitting book, he massively documented the

15

failure of nearly every American school in existence today as resulting not from a planned conspiracy against children but rather from a rigid mindlessness in teachers, administrators, and parents, all obsessed with order and the imposition of a political, psychological jailhouse atmosphere in the typical classroom.

We are now seeking workable models—and not just educational theories—to show how schools can once again become places of purposeful self-renewal in a joyous, happy atmosphere. Fortunately, we now have some models to follow in our pursuit of this goal. One of them, Philadelphia's most publicized Parkway Program, is the major subject of this book.

In June, 1970, the Parkway Program was called by *Philadelphia Magazine* the "biggest splash of the century" in a generally stagnant school system, and *Time,* on March 23, 1970, called it "the most interesting high school in the U.S. today." In May, 1969, *Life* called it the "most radical of all current high school experiments." These are only a few of the encomiums being heaped upon this young and innovative Philadelphia educational program.

If nothing else, the Parkway Program is showing the doubters that there is a workable alternative to the present broken down educational system. There is irresistible magic in any educational institution that can relieve overcrowding and at the same time save money. Already the Parkway is a leading symbol of the new reform movement in education that is emerging on our educational landscape.

In its annual education review, published on January 11, 1971, *The New York Times* headlined an article "Reform Drive Now Key Issue in Education." A key to this reform movement is the "informal" or "open" classroom approach as practiced in the British Infant Schools, Philadelphia's Parkway Program, and in other like-minded pilot institutions.

Silberman pointed out in his *Crisis in the Classroom* that the Parkway Program in Philadelphia is one of the few high schools in the country that is in the process of rediscovering its chief reason for existence. He mentioned only two other high schools that stood out in the small handful of American secondary educational institutions that could be looked upon as innovative models of the future. One was the Newton, Massachusetts, High School and the other was the John Adams High School in Portland, Oregon. By early 1970 Silberman had concluded that: "None as yet can be judged a success; they are still too new and too tentative and experimental (the oldest, at this writing, is in its third year of operation, the youngest, in its first) for any such judgments to be made." (Significantly, he gave more space— seven pages—to his analysis of the Parkway's potential than to any of the others.)[1]

But he strongly suggested that these three schools demanded close study because "of the seriousness with which they are raising fundamental questions about both the means and ends of education." Of the three, he selected the Parkway Program first and gave it the most emphasis, since the architects of the "school without walls" are "questioning virtually every one of the traditional assumptions about what constitutes a school, and what constitutes an education."[2]

The story of the Parkway Program, however, cannot be properly presented in a vacuum. To understand its development, one has to have also an understanding of the political and social milieu surrounding its inception, otherwise a partially distorted picture would result. For this reason, various sections of this book will have rather heavy political overtones.

One of the great myths about the history of American public education is that since "education" is not mentioned anywhere in our U.S. Constitution, it has been blessed for over a century by an almost total divorce from politics. This myth was intensified by separately elected or appointed nonpartisan school boards who have served without pay to keep our schools running.

In recent years, however, particularly since the passage of the watershed national legislation, the Elementary and Secondary Education Act of 1965, this myth has rapidly eroded. In the late sixties, education scholars, such as Professor Ralph Kimbrough, Dean of Educational Administration at the University of Florida, have researched and analyzed this sensitive issue and have concluded that education and politics have never been separated.[3]

[1] Charles E. Silberman, *Crisis in the Classroom* (New York: Random House, Inc., 1970), p. 349.

[2] *Ibid.*

[3] See Ralph Kimbrough, "Power Structures and Educational Change," *Planning and Effecting Needed Changes in Education* in *Designing Education for the Future,* an 8-State Project, Denver, Col., June, 1967, pp. 115-142.

Actually, beginning with the Northwest Ordinance of 1787, in which Congress set aside a certain amount of land for public schools and colleges in each state, education has found itself interwoven with the changes in the political atmosphere of the city, state, and country.

The story of the Parkway Program is no exception. Born in a highly charged political-educational arena in the fourth largest city of the nation, which had neglected the proper education of its children for over a quarter of a century, the Parkway Program symbolized the epitome of the educational renaissance in Philadelphia. It was and still serves as the capstone of a reform movement that has already had serious national repercussions for the future of American education for the balance of this century.

1. Cliff Brenner's Dream —The Incubation of Philadelphia's Parkway Program

"I would not give a penny to the present administrators, and I would largely dismantle the present school machinery."

Paul Goodman [1]

In the late fall of 1967, Clifford Brenner, the Director of Development for the School District of Philadelphia, was charged with the task of finding an alternative solution to reduce secondary school overcrowding rather than to build expensive multimillion dollar high schools. With several of the large city high schools already operating on a dual-session basis and the prospects of more following suit in the years ahead, the necessity of finding a practical equivalent for a 2400 student high school plant, *without* committing the school district to an 18 million dollar capital expenditure in new buildings and land—plus the four- to five-year incubation time—was obvious to Brenner.

As he sat in his second-floor office in the gray-stone, School Board headquarters "castle" located at Twenty-first Street and the Benjamin Franklin Parkway, the development director looked out the window at the Rodin Sculpture Museum across the picturesque grass and tree-lined thoroughfares, and suddenly an idea came to him. In the mile and a half stretch of Philadelphia's famed Parkway, named after her most renowned citizen, over half a dozen cultural institutions were located. "Isn't it possible to somehow utilize this conglomerate of buildings as a linear school without walls?" Brenner reasoned.

Commencing with the historic Philadelphia Art Museum located in Fairmount Park at the head of the Parkway, the 8000-foot long

[1] From an interview with the author.

19

stretch also included such scientific centers as the Franklin Institute, with its Fels Planetarium, the Academy of Natural Sciences, and such humanistic-oriented centers as the main branch of the Free Library of Philadelphia and the Moore School of Art, all around beautiful Logan Circle.

At the lower end of the Parkway, the imposing Victorian edifice of Philadelphia's City Hall, crowned with its statue of William Penn, the founder of the city, stood flanked by the ultramodern Municipal Services Building, the main branch of the YMCA, the Gas Works, the Pennsylvania Bell Telephone Company headquarters, the rust-colored Pennwalt Chemical office building and the Insurance Company of North America building.

Brenner knew that both the Franklin Institute and the Academy of Natural Sciences had been running some small, low-keyed, cooperative science-education programs, mainly for elementary school children, during the past several years. He also knew that the facilities of these institutions (i.e., the classrooms, auditorium, planetarium, etc.) were not being utilized to their maximum capacity during the school day.

As the chief and little publicized theoretician behind the Parkway idea, Brenner had long been seeking ways to relieve overcrowding in the Philadelphia school system. Still in his mid-forties, he had previously successfully negotiated, on behalf of the School Board, the lease of the Cedarwood Unit of Temple University for $1 per year to serve as an outlet for the congestion at the nearby Germantown High School. He was the first person in the top administration of the School Board to recommend and succeed in renting a local synagogue's classroom facilities for public use. (Previously, only local Protestant and Catholic churches had entered into contracts with the School Board to make their Sunday school rooms, equipment, and facilities available for Get-Set prekindergarten uses.)

He also had quietly conducted a feasibility study of the potential educational uses of federal facilities scattered around the city. These moves on the part of Brenner paved the way for his positive formulation of the Parkway concept.

Brenner was confident that the Parkway idea could attract both public and political support. He also felt that major educational foundation support would be forthcoming if the proper approach was made to fund his idea.

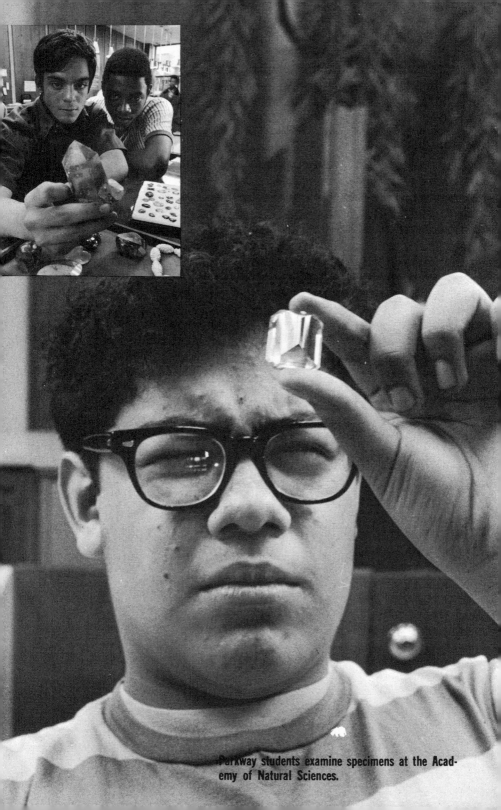

Parkway students examine specimens at the Academy of Natural Sciences.

He first discussed his idea with his superior, Graham Finney, the Deputy Superintendent for Planning. He also talked with several other leading citizens who were sympathetic to the reform movement under Richardson Dilworth's leadership in the Board of Education. One of these was John Patterson, the former chairman of the citizens' educational task forces which were established prior to the Dilworth Board's takeover in January, 1966. Another was Natalie Sachs, an activist citizen expeditor, who possessed a skill in knowing how best to "sell the idea" to the local power structure. These two and others were excited over the prospects of bringing Brenner's dream into reality at an early date.

In late 1967, with their advice, Brenner rewrote his original memo to Finney and discussed its contents informally with Dilworth before it was formally presented to the entire nine-member board. He also took his plan to Dr. Mark Shedd, the Superintendent of Schools, through the proper administrative channels, and received an enthusiastic reception from him.

Brenner realized that most good educational ideas were synthesized from others who had come before, and he was the first to admit his debt to earlier educators. (Brenner did *not* conceive of his plan as purely a quick and cheap education space outlet for overcrowding, but rather based it on his own academic and philosophical background in the educational field. He is a former high school math teacher.

Without consulting the authorities in charge of these private, nonprofit cultural institutions on the Parkway as to whether they would be willing to cooperate with the school district of Philadelphia in undertaking such a novel and innovative program, Brenner presented his proposal to the School Board and the administrative staff in late December, 1967. Most of his administrative colleagues and the Board approved the concept and agreed with him that the semipublic, sister institutions dotting the Parkway would probably be attracted to the idea when they were formally approached to cooperate in the plan.

The next major step leading to the birth of the Parkway Program occurred in March, 1968, when Shedd and his Board held a press conference with the heads of the neighboring cultural and business institutions along and near the Benjamin Franklin Parkway to announce the potential cooperative educational uses of their joint resources.

Following this conference, a small advisory committee was established to keep the Parkway school-without-walls idea alive, so that the eventual educational manager of the Program would be able to inherit something more than a few ideas scrawled on a piece of paper. Clifford Brenner was picked for that committee along with Joel Bloom, the Director of Science Education for the Franklin Institute, located just across the street from the School Board headquarters; John Patterson; and a representative from the Archdiocesan Schools of Philadelphia.

Their task was to recruit and hire a permanent Executive Director of the Program, and with the help of Mario Fantini of the Ford Foundation, they found Dr. John Bremer. Fantini knew of Bremer's desire to leave the Ford-sponsored Two Bridges experimental school district in Lower Manhattan and could vouch for Bremer's creativity and ability. Shedd's role was to facilitate the bringing of Bremer, an outsider, on board by acting as the coordinator and midwife of the project.

Mark Shedd was then given Board approval to apply to the Ford Foundation for a grant to fund the incubation period of the project, to bring the concept to fruition as soon as possible, and to hire Bremer. (Less than a year later, with the aid of a gift of $100,000 from Ford Foundation to carry the project through its first year, the Parkway School was able to open its many doors to its first group of students—a feat heretofore unheard of in the annals of American public education.)

Ironically, the three key men involved in the birth of the Parkway Program—Brenner, Bremer, and Shedd—were all in their early forties at the time of their involvement with the planning and the initial operation of the innovative educational effort. Since the Parkway concept was a new idea, it was natural that educators who were young in age and mind should play a vital role in its birth.

Bremer, the guiding Pied Piper behind the original operation of the Parkway School, was a cherubic, shaggy-haired, happy-go-lucky British educational import. The then forty-two-year-old director of the new Parkway school came to Philadelphia in August, 1968, from New York City where he had been the superintendent of the Two Bridges experimental, decentralized community school district. It was one of three such districts in the city, of which the Ocean Hill-Brownsville district was the most controversial, because it was at the core of the long teachers' strike in the fall of 1968.

Bremer started his career up the educational ladder in a one-room school back in 1946. After obtaining graduate degrees at the University of Leicester (in his hometown), St. John's College, Tavistock Institute of Human Relations, and the University of Cambridge, Bremer came to the United States in 1951 as a Fulbright Fellow. He later became a professor at the Brooklyn Center of Long Island University and at the New School for Social Research in New York.

Returning to England in 1962, this blonde, bespectacled educator spent the next four years as a professor in the University of Leicester's Graduate School of Education, where he worked with prospective and practicing teachers in the Leicestershire Plan schools which were developing new methods of teacher training and new approaches to student learning.

Part of Bremer's educational philosophy which lay under the planning of the Parkway Program envisioned the learning dimensions of the students as not being restricted to "special places called classrooms, or in special buildings called schools." Rather, he said in an interview, "It is a quality appropriate to any and every phase of human existence, or, more strictly, it is human life itself." (Shades of John Dewey!)

"Our schools today imagine that students learn best in a special building or 'box' separated from the larger community," explained Bremer. "This has created a refuge in which students do not need to explore but only to accept."

The student's learning is evaluated within the "boxes" and it is never tested against the realities of life. Bremer continued, "It is a common feeling that what is learned is only for the purposes of the school and this is the well-known irrelevance of education." It is not possible, Bremer believed, to improve the high school as we know it. "It has reached the end of its development. What is needed," he concluded, "is a new kind of education institution. In the Parkway Program, we will study the city in the city. Since our lives are inseparable from the city, it is our campus and our curriculum."

"Our system was a success in its time," Bremer conceded in answer to the question of what was wrong with the old way, "but the times are different now." "If education is the mechanism by which the child becomes an adult," Bremer stated, "then we must update the mechanism by which today's updated child will become the updated adult in this time."

"Every age had its crucial problems. Ours is coping with change," he said, explaining the "Why" of the much-discussed experiment in education.

The question we must ask, Bremer went on, is "Can we devise an educational system that copes with change?" To Bremer, the Parkway Project is just such a system.

He sees the role of an educational system as "one that produces an orderly, happy, useful citizen of his society." To do this, the educational system must teach the student the skills that are basic to producing the orderly, happy, useful citizen. The Project, as developed by Bremer and his staff, is a middle ground between what the student wants and what he needs. "It is our goal to develop the basic skills through media that he wants," said Bremer.

The Parkway idea which Bremer kept insisting is not a "school" but a "program" departs from the old-fashioned concepts of what constitutes formal education in a number of ways. The absence of any one central building or campus is foremost among these characteristics. This means that boundaries of the educational process surrounding the Parkway Program parallel the "life space of the student himself," according to Bremer.

The Parkway Program was thus aimed at helping the student to adapt and learn within his present life space and to help him expand that space, including all aspects of the city and the neighboring environs.

Bremer's Parkway manifesto aimed at hastening the end of the old educational order was best summed up when he said: "The days of the school system as a triangle, with the superintendent at the apex, have gone. The new geometrical figure is a circle with the work task—*learning*—at the center and with the total community on the circumference. For all of us—student or superintendent, principal or parent, taxpayer or teacher—are equidistant from that work task, and nobody can claim priority."

Mark Shedd pointed out that another issue facing the Parkway's advisory committee, besides selecting a director, was to find ways to structure the program in advance, including the practical aspects of management. Bremer's insistence that the program be completely "unstructured" created the first signs of friction between himself and his superior. "He wanted to plan from the ground up," Shedd reflected in a conversation, "and he ultimately had his way, for the most part." (Shedd later felt that Bremer could have compromised more than he did with his superiors in his adamant desire to have a free rein in setting up the program.)

So, even before the Parkway dream became a reality, some ripples had appeared that would later churn up the waters of discontent between two strong-willed educators.

Mortimer Smith, the Executive Director of the Council for Basic Education, had postulated that the "philosophical battle over change in our schools seems to be shaping up between the old-line critics, who believe that the schools have failed in their principal function of intellectual training, and the new romantic radicals, whose interest lies more in emotional and social development than in intellectual attainment."

He did not include John Bremer, the first director of Philadelphia's Parkway Program, who was a relative newcomer on the American educational scene as one of the "romantic radicals," but the English-born educator would fit easily into this category, which includes such names as the aforementioned Goodman, Holt, Kozol, Postman, and Silberman. Since the foundation of the Parkway Program was patterned after the educational romanticists' and reformers' emphasis on the students' feelings and the need for joy in the educational process, this school without walls fits nicely into the romantic education category.

We have now come full circle from the post-World War II emphasis on making the school system more intellectually vigorous under the tutelage of such disciplined, basic education-oriented leaders as Vice Admiral Hyman Rickover, Professors Arthur Bestor, James Conant, and Jerrold Zacharias. These men, who were subject-matter centered in their thinking, played their influential role in the late forties and fifties, only to find their influence waning in the late sixties as the combined impact of the civil rights' revolution, Sputnik, and the hippie revolution took their toll and spilled their libertarian trends over onto the college and high school campuses of the nation.

This push of outside forces helped to set the stage for the birth of the Parkway Program that was not long in coming.

2. Before the Parkway Everything Added Up to Add

"To a very great degree, school is a place where children learn to be stupid."
                                        John Holt [1]

The story of the Philadelphia schools in the mid-twentieth century revolves around the machinations of a little-known tyrant who almost single-handedly wrecked the system. His name was Add Burke Anderson.

Within a short period after his death in harness at the age of sixty-four (on August 15, 1962), the memory of this former $24,500 business manager and secretary of the School Board, who dictatorially ran the system for twenty-eight years, was honored by the Board with a new elementary school dedicated in his name. The late Brigadier General J. Harry LeBrum, (USA, ret.) the Board president, eulogized the tenth-grade dropout from Central High with these words: "He [Add] ate, drank and slept the School District. He is almost an irreparable loss."

Anderson started as a $5-a-day office boy at the school district headquarters back in 1915, and after nineteen years of doing jobs that no one else wanted, he worked himself up to the post of Director of Non-Instructional Services and Supplies (in charge of janitors, etc.) and then Business Manager in 1934, although he had no college training for the post. From this position, he slowly expanded the tentacles of his power by making political deals with the soft coal barons of Lackawanna County who sat in the legislature at Harrisburg. He would make an annual trek to the state capitol and extract a promise of a meager state supplement

[1] John Holt, *How Children Fail* (New York: Pitman Publishing Corporation, 1969), p. 157.

to his two-page school budget (that he always kept locked in his desk) in return for a quid pro quo that all new schools would be built with boilers that would burn only Pennsylvania bituminous coal (at increased expense to the Philadelphia taxpayers).

Anderson was violently opposed to the federal school lunch program to feed 160,000 hungry ghetto children, since he felt that it would cost the school district hard cash to cook the free food on its school stoves.

A champion of the school janitors, firemen, and tree-trimmers, who made more money than the teachers, he threatened school principals who resisted his policies by denying them vital supplies with which to operate.

A man of economy, he said that the Board could save more than $10 million over a ten-year period by firing all the experienced teachers and hiring beginning ones. In 1939 the South Philadelphia Branch of the Communist Party had him arrested for criminal libel. He was accused of saying that the Reds planned to burn down some city schools. Add was freed by a friendly magistrate, but the news accounts of the incident with his photo emblazoned across page one made him wince. "The picture really made me look like a criminal," he said sadly.

Anderson was a bald, dull, thin-lipped businessman. In 1958, when he had a fainting spell at the age of sixty and took a temporary leave of absence, things got very confused at the School Board until he got back to his desk.

For over twenty years, Anderson ran the school system of Philadelphia, which lent credence to the saying that at the School Board during his tenure, "Everything added up to Add." A summary in the *Philadelphia Magazine* of the strategy and tactics of this tight-fisted business manager concluded: "However, did a ward leader have a constituent in need of a job? Call Add. The school board always had room for one more. Did City Council have a favorite architect or builder? Add would be more than happy to consider him. . . ." [2]

Add ran a quiet ship, but the school system continued to rot under policies set by him until a new superintendent, Dr. C. Taylor Whittier, was appointed by an interim School Board in 1964. The first move that Whittier made when he took office was to put the business manager back under the control of the superin-

[2] "See Mark Shedd Run," *Philadelphia Magazine,* June, 1969, p. 76.

tendent. But this act did not bring about the necessary reforms that were sorely needed to breathe new life into the moth-eaten school system.

At the time of Anderson's death, the last superintendent to suffer under Add's rule, Allen Wetter, commented piously: "I never knew anyone who contributed more to the progress of the Philadelphia school system than Add B. Anderson." Add indirectly set the stage for the birth of the Parkway Program by his tight budget policy which forced most of the existing high school plants in the city to go to double shifts in order to serve all of the student demands.

Some critics have said that the moribund Philadelphia school system had continued to slumber in the nineteenth-century educational doldrums until the dynamic and charismatic ex-Mayor Richardson Dilworth in early 1966 took over the School Board that had been largely dominated for decades by puppets of the business community. The Board had been conveniently selected for their posts over the years by sympathetic Common Pleas Court judges. The people had no voice in selecting the Board. One of the Board members had served for over twenty-five years.

When Dilworth found Dr. Mark Shedd, thirty-nine, in the small town of Englewood, New Jersey, the silver-haired, septuagenarian patrician was hoping that the young school administrator could clean out the bureaucratic deadwood that had accumulated at the Parkway headquarters of the school district.

After Shedd, in September, 1967, became the thirteenth school superintendent in Philadelphia's history, his much heralded dynamic personality and expertise were soon found to have some serious flaws. He had no sense of humor and his coolness often turned people off. When it came time to pick his reform team to aid him in the revolution, he disappointed many hopeful observers by selecting old Add Anderson holdovers for the key administrative posts. He left the Old Establishment intact, particularly in the curriculum and field operations departments.

This situation was to have a deleterious effect on the prospects for a smooth liaison with Dr. John Bremer when he arrived to take over the Parkway Program, since the new administrator in town had to deal not only with his boss, Shedd, but also with a skeptical and somewhat antagonistic bureaucracy who really did not take to this foreign upstart coming in to shake up the system.

29

In this first in-depth analysis ever made of the City of Brotherly Love's public school system, Henry Resnik, a free-lance journalist who taught for a time in the Pennsylvania Advancement School, praised Shedd and his colleagues for their attempts to bring a fresh activist style to his office, "Anti-authoritarianism was at the heart of this style;" wrote Resnik, "it was resolutely democratic. It emphasized the values of community, honesty, and trust, and it was more concerned with the emotions than with the intellect." [3]

This philosophy provided a naturally conducive atmosphere for experimentation with new, innovative approaches to help break the lockstep and stultifying barriers of the rigidly operated system. The Parkway concept fitted in nicely with this thinking. Yet, as time passed, even before the birth of the Parkway Program, Resnik's vision of the libertarian approaches began to blur, and he became disillusioned with slow progress of the Shedd/Dilworth revolution.

He did not examine the Parkway Program in his volume, since his book went to press before he had time to analyze its early impact. Speaking of allied local experimental educational projects like the Advancement School, Resnik gave a hint of rocky things to come when he expounded on the actions of some of the "good guys" in the school system. "As innovation became a cliché instead of a goal," he discovered, "a rivalry for newness turned many program leaders into prima donnas of change. . . . Often it seemed that a commitment to humanism was merely another trick, a subtle mask covering a lust for power." [4]

Resnik's indictment marked a fairly accurate preview of events that were to affect seriously Dr. John Bremer before he had completed two years of his tenure as head of the Parkway Project. Meantime, Shedd had withdrawn into a semishell and had become increasingly uncommunicative with the public and his staff as his dreams of making Philadelphia the Number One big city school system in the nation slowly crumbled around him.

[3] Henry S. Resnik, *Turning on the System* (New York: Pantheon Books, A Division of Random House, Inc., 1970), p. 58.
[4] *Ibid.*, pp. 24 and 25.

3. The Birth of Alpha in an Old Bank Loft

"The moral purpose of education is universal and dominant in all instruction—whatsoever the topic."   John Dewey [1]

The magnetic appeal of the Parkway idea was based on at least nine individualistic and outstanding characteristics. These characteristics of what makes Parkway special are:

- no school building or classrooms
- courses offered all around the city
- students help hire and evaluate teachers
- students aid in curriculum planning
- student-faculty "management" groups run the program
- no formal discipline or dress code
- students selected randomly by lottery
- business and industry contribute some teachers
- cost per student less than average cost in Philadelphia school system.

These important features set the Parkway apart from other recent educational "experiments." The public nature of the program, which was fully accredited and supported by the school district, and the commitment to operate the program at cost equal to or less than the amount required to run a traditional school were other important supporting characteristics.

The question underlying the Program's foundation was whether or not the resources of the urban community, concentrated in one geographical area, could be used to the educational advantage of a broad cross section of secondary school students. Part of

[1] John Dewey, *Moral Principles in Education,* as quoted in Silberman, *Crisis in the Classroom,* p. 9.

31

Group of students and local businessmen discuss careers at Alpha Branch in old bank loft.

the challenge of this question was the assumption that for the surrounding community institutions to accept the students into their organizations, the Parkway students would have to learn to operate differently than they did in their former school situations.

The structure of the Parkway then was not just to expose the students to the community but to meet the demands of that community and in some cases to help bring social change to the community from below instead of from above.

During the last days of the hectic, preplanning period in early 1969, the prospects for the Parkway School were brightened by an unexpected windfall, the expansion of its initial student population pool to include seven more students coming in from outside the city limits. This fact made the Parkway School the first truly urban-suburban, joint-metro school in the Delaware Valley. The events leading up to this prenatal good news for Bremer and his staff were as follows.

For several years, Philadelphia's School Board President Dilworth had been making many public relations pilgrimages to the surrounding bedroom counties of Montgomery, Bucks, Delaware, and Chester, trying to convince their residents of the need to establish a regional, metropolitan school system. Until the opening of the Parkway School in February, 1969, he had no takers since the fear of the liabilities of forced reverse bussing of suburban school children to the city ghetto schools usually overcame the assets accruing from the establishment of an enlarged educational system.

Then the miracle happened. Just one week before the opening of the new school on the Parkway, several enterprising parents from neighboring, affluent Cheltenham, located just across the city line from the northeast section of Philadelphia, pressured their local school board to allow some of their children to attend the new institution. The parents had already made application to enroll their children in the Parkway School with the full knowledge that they were competing with requests from children and parents coming from over a dozen other public and parochial suburban school districts who were all vying for the privilege of having some of their children fill a portion of the thirty openings allotted to non-city school children.

The Cheltenham School Board voted unanimously in mid-

February to become the first suburban district to allow "six or seven" of its high school students to attend the new school on a tuition-free exchange basis. This mutual cooperative gesture meant that these pioneer "foreign" students could enroll in the Parkway School without paying the $680-a-year tuition fee for outsiders in return for permission being granted to Philadelphia to send a half dozen of its students to attend Cheltenham High School on a reciprocal basis. This type of "reverse" student bussing definitely had a positive appeal to some of the more enlightened suburbs!

At 9:00 A.M. on Monday, February 17, 1969, a ninth grade class composed of 143 public and parochial students, met with the project's director, Dr. John Bremer, and the faculty in the newly converted second floor rented loft of an old bank building located on busy Market Street—several blocks from the Parkway. The first unit was named "Alpha" by Bremer, signifying the first letter in the classical Greek alphabet. Future units were to be named "Beta," "Gamma," etc. Future plans called for an escalation of the number of students to 400 in the fall of 1969 with a full four-year class in residence by that time.

The first ungraded class of the Parkway School, selected at random by drawing names from over 2200 applications submitted through the eight school districts and the archdiocese, showed a fairly even racially balanced makeup of 68 black students (48%) to 75 white students (52%). Fifteen were selected from each of the districts and twenty from the parochial and suburban schools. Since some districts are almost all black and others predominantly white in a public school system that is now 59 percent black, this heterogeneous breakdown represented a fairly accurate cross section of the city's school population. The student IQs ranged from 74 to 150.

Why was this approach used instead of a "first-come, first-served" or an aptitude test means of selection? Bremer explained: "First, we are an educational program and the best of what we have to offer is freely available to any public school student. We are not the private preserve of any racial, social, economic, or professional group, and, if we were, it would be impossible for us to be an educational program at all simply because the students would then be the instruments of somebody else's purposes, that is, of the purposes of that special group. But in education, the student is always the end, never a means.

34

"Second, if we were not willing to admit any and every student, we would have to set what are called admissions standards. In my opinion, admissions standards are a method of discrimination —not as is often pretended on the basis of scientifically established criteria—but on the basis of social criteria. To use them would be to destroy the community in which alone education can take place.

"Third, the prime object of the study of life—what we learn— must always, in some way, be useful to us in life. Now our lives are urban lives, not suburban lives, but urban lives. The city is life; it is where the action is. But Philadelphia is a city, is *one* city, only insofar as it belongs to all of us, and it can never belong to all of us if it is the curriculum for an elite, for some select group.

"Fourth, by adopting our method, all students, whether admitted now or not, learn the most fundamental of lessons—that we can relate to one another on the basis of love and honesty. It is, perhaps, small comfort for those not now admitted, but such students are better off than if they had been admitted by dishonest, discriminatory, or corrupt means. And if we had been dishonest and admitted them, what would our love now be worth?"

During the three weeks' orientation period, the students were at first divided into nine tutorial groups of about fifteen each with two staff members assigned to each unit. The tutorial group is one in which the student works on the basic skills required for a diploma, is given remedial or advanced work, and receives counsel from his teachers. The pupil-teacher ratio is ideal when compared with the overcrowded classes in the public and parochial schools which average thirty-five to one. During the orientation sessions, students were counseled about the various opportunities in the forty-five different specialized courses that they might pursue in the Parkway institutions. The tutorial sessions also gave the students and teachers a chance to evaluate the program.

Following the first week's orientation program, the 143 students and their teachers walked across Market Street to see the Italian-made film version of *Romeo and Juliet,* after which they came back to their seminar classrooms to discuss Franco Zeffirelli's contemporary cinematic approach to Shakespeare. This experience in the educational uses of artistic commercial cinema was followed by a visit to the school district's headquarters' auditorium two days later to view a poignant, amateur-made film called *The Jungle*. This latter film was produced in the summer of 1968 in the heart of Philadelphia's black ghetto by a group of juveniles representing the Twelfth and Oxford Street gang. It depicted life in the raw in that deprived section of the city as seen through the eyes of the participants.

These early field trips were part of a special, four-day study unit on the Urban Environment, which included discussions on love, hate, and intergroup relationships in the city. At the completion of this training period in early March, the students moved out to the twenty-five cooperating scientific, cultural, social, and business institutions on the Parkway and its environs, where they planned to become involved in the interdisciplinary areas of their choice.

A typical school day at the Parkway educational complex looks like this:

From 9:00 to 11:00 A.M., the student has a choice of visiting a local business or one of the cultural centers either on his own or in a group with a faculty member escort. From 11:00 A.M. to 1:00 P.M., he may join a "management group" to eat his lunch. (The management groups, treat such topics as self-government, fund raising, athletics, public relations, the Constitution, etc.) From 1:00 to 3:00 P.M., he can join one of eight tutorial units where he receives instruction in the normal, state-mandated high school curriculum so that he can qualify for college entrance requirements. From 3:00 to 5:00 P.M., he might again visit one of the institutions on the newly baptized "Pedagogical Mile," the invisible school without walls on the Parkway.

On Wednesdays, from 11:00 A.M. to 5:00 P.M., the student is free to participate in special activities or individual study. On Friday, between 1:00 and 3:00 P.M., he participates in a mandatory seminar to discuss what he has learned in the various centers. The program lacks the rigidity of regular school curricula, and the typical student will be responsible for traveling from one of his self-chosen activities to another via walking or ultimately a special Parkway School-Shuttle Minibus which will make frequent trips up and down the route connecting the cooperating institutions to speed up student movement. Public transportation is also used.

The Parkway student is asked to choose his own curriculum from four different categories of subjects.

The subjects—"offerings" are what the Project calls them—to be chosen are a combination of basics that are required by state law and electives that are designed to capture the interest of the young people and prepare them for what they want to do.

The "basic skills" courses offer the old standbys of "reading, 'riting, and 'rithmetic." But there are such incongruous subjects as Shakespeare, Chaucer, and contemporary black writers; "Feelings and Ideas"; "Computers"; "Business Mathematics"; "Mathematics"; and "Mathematics for Science."

If the more traditionally minded reject teaching such things as computers and business math, what will they think of such electives as "Vagabond Sketching," "Go Fly a Kite," "Filmmaking," and "Maggots, Mosquitoes, and Mice"? But before one leaps to conclusions that the electives are frivolous, consider: "Music," "How City Planning Works," "Urban Economics," "The American Trade Union Movement," "Introduction to Physical Chemistry"; or "Multimedia Journalism," "Unpopular Philosophy," "Market Research," "Business Skills for Beginning Jobs"; or "You and Art," "Drama Workshop," "Aspects of African Culture"; or French, Spanish, Latin, Italian, Hebrew, Swahili, Russian, German, Polish, and Greek.

The student's schedule must include at least one choice—and more if he can fit them in—from among such "institutional offerings" as "The Modern Corporation," "Biology Seminars," "Law Enforcement," and "Printing."

Some of the other initial possibilities for student selection from among ninety course offerings and specialization could be found in the peculiar diverse characteristics of the cooperating institutions. Mathematics are taught at the Franklin Institute, English and literature at the Main Branch of the Free Library, statistics at the insurance building, art appreciation at the Art Museum and the Rodin Museum, physics and chemistry at the Franklin Institute, biology at the Academy of Natural Sciences, physical education at the YMCA, social studies at the Youth Study Center, and zoology and anthropology at the Philadelphia Zoo in nearby Fairmount Park.

All of the above named institutions, plus such nearby, non-Parkway enterprises as Smith Kline and French pharmaceutical laboratories, the *Philadelphia Inquirer* and *The Evening Bulletin* newspaper buildings, and the KYW-NBC radio and TV studios, agreed to participate in this offbeat educational program. Philadelphia's city hall, the police station, and the county court building, where a special course in law enforcement is taught by a young law graduate working as an assistant district attorney, also opened their doors to Parkway students.

Besides the secular institutions already cited, the Parkway Program is unique in the utilization of unused neighboring church facilities. The more than a dozen churches that offered their Sunday school rooms and other facilities to the Parkway Program in the Center City area were mostly Protestant. There were few Roman Catholic churches or Jewish synagogues nearby—except for the main Catholic edifice, the Cathedral of Ss. Peter and Paul, on the Parkway's Logan Circle—which could have served the program. The latter, however, was the parish church of John Cardinal Krol, and as a hard-line Catholic educator, he did not look upon the Parkway Program with much favoritism. In fact, in its first three years of existence, he never once made a public statement in support of the program, although his chief educational deputy, Monsignor Edward Hughes, the Archdiocesan Superintendent of Schools, did make several statements of support for this ecumenical educational effort which included students from the public and parochial urban school systems.

Those Protestant churches which did cooperate with the program, like the First Unitarian Church at Twenty-second and Chestnut Streets, never had any major complaints about the Parkway students abusing their church property. In fact, most of them found it financially advantageous to sign contracts with the Parkway and School Board officials since the rental income, though small, helped these churches with declining parishes over some budgetary problems of their own.

The Philadelphia precedent for the use of churches for the Parkway Program had been set three years earlier when the school district quietly entered into contracts with some twenty-eight Protestant and Catholic churches as well as several synagogues, mainly in the North Philadelphia ghetto area, to use their Sunday school rooms during the day for Head Start and Get-Set nursery school programs. These arrangements were made possible by federal money flowing into the city after the dual passage of the Equal Opportunities Act of 1964 and the Elementary and Secondary Education Act of 1965.

The Parkway Program is unusual not only in the physical facilities provided for the youngsters, but also in the extent of student involvement in the program's overall management.

Students make their own decisions about the subjects they want to study, designing their curriculum to include courses, like photography and filmmaking, as they go along. They also have an equal voice with the program's administrators in selecting their teachers, and they regularly attend Friday morning faculty meetings.

In keeping with the casual air that surrounds the school, students call teachers by their first names. There are no formal discipline codes and no dress or hair regulations.

But in spite of the Parkway's apparent free-wheeling atmosphere, Bremer insisted, the program is actually tightly structured. Students, he felt, spend more time studying than their counterparts from regular high schools. The school day lasts from nine to five for many of the program's youngsters, with special Saturday classes.

Although plans call for increasing student enrollment, the basic structure of the program is still expected to remain the same—with enrollment continuously siphoned into units of approximately 150 students each.

During the shakedown semester, the Alpha Unit of the Parkway Program utilized a staff of eighteen assisting Bremer—nine fully certified teachers, with from one to twelve years' experience; and nine university interns, seven from Antioch College in Ohio and two from the University of Massachusetts. From the varied interests and backgrounds of this young volunteer faculty, which was equally balanced ethnically, came the wide assortment of courses which was offered to the students.

The Parkway faculty encourages its students to participate in individual study programs with one or two other students. Students also are given the opportunity to enter the work programs which can lead to vacation jobs or career possibilities.

Students receive only pass or fail grades, but evaluation of their performance is, nonetheless, an important part of the process. At the end of each semester, students and teachers are involved in a two-week evaluation which takes place in the tutorial groups. The faculty evaluates the student's progress and each student evaluates his own progress and that of the faculty. A form is sent home to parents asking them also to evaluate their child's growth in the program.

Although a number of parents were doubtful at first, Bremer recalled, reactions up to now have been "enormously favorable."

Most of the students and teachers appear to be enthusiastic. Some students, for example, call the program a "school for kids," an epithet the staff evaluates as the highest form of flattery. An informal survey indicates that roughly one-third haa plans to drop out of their original high schools. But only one youngster left the Parkway Program during the first semester.

Initially, the teachers praised the flexibility and freedom the program offered to utilize experimental methods and a variety of places to meet, but admit that the Parkway could use some "stabilizing." A definite weak point, as far as teachers are concerned, is the poor intra-staff communication that often accompanies the flexibility.

"Teachers just don't know what's going on all the time because of so many changes in plans or schedules," said one staff member. "For example, one time we weren't even aware of a news conference being held about the program."

Teachers also were concerned about what one faculty member called a "lack of genuine, across-the-board interaction between black and white students after class. Parkway students come from very different areas of the city and socially they seem to feel that it's safer to go with people they already know."

Apart from these criticisms, however, the Philadelphia Board of Education, for one, was sufficiently impressed by the program early in its first year to take over its funding for the 1970-71 school year from the Ford Foundation.

How do the students take to this national attention-getting experiment?

They learned early that they were part of a community of their own making. They upheld a belief that Bremer had held, that a person "can't belong to a community unless he can make a contribution to it." It may be a small thing, but Bremer was proud of the fact that except for three instances on the first day, there has been no disfigurement of the walls and property of the main building at 1801 Market St. "They realized very quickly," Bremer said, "that it is their community and their problem."

This awareness has resulted in a similar involvement with regard to the offerings that each student selected. To the graduate of the "old school," however, there may be some doubts when he observes a class in action. To the comment that "none of our teachers would have permitted so much noise," Bremer replied that language begins with talking and that if you are going to have learning, you are going to have noise.

Despite the initial enthusiasm for the Parkway by its chief consumers, the students, the same could not be said by its future holders of the purse strings, the politicians in the city, who were in a position to undermine or support the effort. After the Parkway Program had been under way for one month, one of the more powerful Democratic city councilmen announced that he and the mayor were suspicious of two of the School Board's projects—the Parkway effort and the Pennsylvania Advancement School (another Ford-sponsored local innovative educational effort). The mayor and some of the council members were angry at School Board President Dilworth for allegedly accusing them of appealing to bigotry and fear in their attacks on the Parkway Program and the Adancement School. The councilmen were having strong second thoughts about the controversial school budget because of the addition of these programs. The council president also lashed out against the Parkway idea, opting for a return to the old-fashioned "neighborhood school" concept instead.

So, the Parkway Program had to struggle during its initial birth pangs not only against the entrenched educational bureaucracy at the School Board headquarters but also against the negative reactions in City Hall, where there was only one councilman, the maverick Democrat, David Cohen, who was willing to speak out in favor of the experiment.

41

4. Beta Comes After Alpha

"What the best and wisest parent wants for his own child, that must the community want for all of its children. Any other idea for our schools is narrow and unlovely; acted upon, it destroys our democracy."   *John Dewey, 1899* [1]

The Parkway Program soon earned a reputation as a fine example of a learning institution that is humane and can educate because it is concerned with gaiety, joy, and individual growth without sacrificing individual discipline and development. Simultaneously, it is child-centered, subject-centered, and teacher-centered.

The Parkway effort soon received national attention in educational circles. Word-of-mouth encomiums spread across the country so that before long, over a dozen requests a day were being processed from V.I.P. local, state, and national educational administrators and school board members who wanted to come and see for themselves what the program was all about.

By mid-1969, the puckish Dr. Bremer proudly stated that the Parkway Project had already proved that there "are a million ways to learn and a million ways to teach." He felt that already this program was a successful experiment in a new type of education which gave the students a chance to create a new order of learning in which cooperation between students had a priority over competition.

In reply to criticisms that he ran a confused, unstructured institution, Bremer retorted, "We are not unstructured. We are just

[1] Martin S. Dworkin, ed., *Dewey on Education* (New York: Bureau of Publications, Teachers College, Columbia University, 1959), p. 34.

structured in a different way which gives our students a share of responsibility for their own freedom and to formulate their own learning experiences."

The philosophy underlying his concept of the Parkway Program was based mainly on the learning theories of a triad of past giants: the Greek, Plato; the Austrian, Sigmund Freud; and the American, John Dewey. Bremer mixed a bit of each of their philosophies into a pedagogical potpourri that resulted in a group of turned-on pupils, most of whom had been turned-off in their former, traditionally structured schools. He also borrowed from A. S. Neill's Summerhill concept, but unlike that fellow-English educator's isolated, rural setting, Bremer felt the Parkway concept is "related to the wider community" and is therefore superior for current urban needs.

Although he agreed that there was some similarity between the Parkway experiment and the Summerhill experiment, Bremer also noted several important differences. The latter, a private school, was predominantly aimed at educating elementary children in the country, while the public, largely secondary school of the Parkway Program was located in the heart of a major city, just across the street from a couple of sleazy, second-run movie theaters, and just down the street from the Greyhound Bus Terminal.

The first Parkway director also leaned heavily on the late Albert North Whitehead's definition that there is only one subject matter for education, and that is "Life" in all its manifestations for his guiding philosophy; along with that of Socrates, who said: "For our conversation is not about something casual, but about the proper way to live." Bremer hoped that the typical Parkway student would really learn how to live with others as well as with himself during his tour at the Parkway.

Dr. Bremer added his own recipe to that of the giants of the past by stressing that great emphasis is needed on the quality of educational relationships among students, teachers, and administrators. This means keeping the learning community small in order to best find the proper and appropriate way in which to live. "Since learning is a human activity," Bremer said, "the problem of how to enter into the learning process, or to be a learner, can be restated in terms of group membership—how to be a member of a learning community."

He deeply believed that this philosophy applied both to teachers

and students. The learning cycle for instructors does not end with the attainment of a college degree and teaching certificate, but is an ongoing affair in which teachers learn along with the students as they teach, and not in special in-service training programs which are the pattern now in most schools.

"Every school should have as part of its own curriculum the continuing re-creation of its own curriculum," Bremer postulated. This is why he pushed for the cooperative venture of students and teachers becoming involved in the constant planning and evaluation of their curricula.

Bremer also based his personal educational theory on the fact that children learn by doing even when they are doing something that society frowns upon, like gambling or playing cards in the school hallways. He even condoned kite flying, if a student desired to participate in that activity. "After all," said Bremer, "let's not forget that Ben Franklin gave kites a big start in this country." He believed that it was more important to get learning started than to talk about goals.

The integrated, randomly selected volunteer student body (55 percent black and 45 percent white) has already shown that more

Student activity may include a field trip in Center City Philadelphia or a photography class.

and better learning could occur in smaller complexes than in the large city high schools with populations running into the thousands. "We do not suffer from the curse of bigness with all its stultifying side-effects," Bremer pointed out. [2]

One reason there has been no significant drug problem plaguing the Parkway student body and student smoking is on the decrease there, according to the director, is "because we have reduced the level of anxiety and hostility here." Bremer also felt that this urban educational experiment provided a beacon to the suburbs because "you can't have a decent education there where the predominantly white student bodies are investing their energies in fighting fear and guilt" in their racially isolated communities.

The twinkle-eyed educator, who wore his long blond, curly hair in a semi-hippie hairdo, stressed the point that "any educational system that says 'This is the *only* way to do something' is bound to fail!"

[2] Quotes from an interview with Dr. Bremer reported in "School Without Walls" by Donald Cox in *Youth,* June 7, 1970. Reprinted with permission of *Youth* magazine, published for teenagers by the United Church Press. Copyright © 1970.

"Our educational problem today," he concluded, "is to set a balance between order and disorder . . . so that we can help America create an educational system worthy of itself."

The excitement that the Parkway Program has generated among its students and faculty is noticed by every visitor who has observed its many educational activities—wherever they are held. From Bremer's own intellectually rigorous classes in Greek and Plato (which drew upon his own classical education back in England) to the informal classes held outdoors, one can't help but be impressed by the enthusiastic atmosphere surrounding the whole program.

Although several students at the Parkway Program had difficulty at first adjusting to the "looseness" of the setting as compared with the strict hierarchical atmosphere of their previous high school, most soon made the transition comfortably. "There's a lot of goofing off here," said one eleventh grader who formerly had been a troublemaker at Olney High, "but they work with you and find out what's bugging you. At my old school, they pretended to care, but they really didn't. They would say: 'You're a smart boy, so wise up!' They didn't get to know what was bugging me though."

"There's so much bull before you learn anything in other schools," observed a fellow student. "There're tardy slips and suspensions for fighting and smoking. You know that sooner or later they are going to get you, so our attitude there was: 'Why go?' So we turned off. We get yelled at at home and in those schools, but here we are much happier."

Some of the Parkway students soon acquired a hidden fear that the Board was seeking to undercut their program and was just waiting to find something wrong so that they could close it down. This extra unwritten incentive has put most of the students on their guard to see that the program does not get any unfavorable publicity, i.e., abuse of other people's and institutional property. This knowledge has worked to the advantage of the program in its early struggles to succeed.

The magnetic attraction of the Parkway Program for teachers who desired to move out of a public school straitjacket into a freer atmosphere was best evidenced by the more than four hundred applications which came in from all over the country for twenty openings during the first year of operation. Prospective teachers were interviewed by parents, students, administrative staff, and university interns who were associated with the project. Most of those who volunteered to go through the tough selection process were young—mostly in their twenties—and had at least a B.A. degree in their chosen field of expertise.

The initial faculty of the Parkway Program were all eager to help pioneer new educational frontiers. Typical of this group of enthusiastic volunteers who made up Bremer's core staff were: Cy Schwartz, a graduate of Philadelphia's prestigious Central High School and Temple University who was interested in film as literature and in training young film makers; James Schuster, who had conducted an in-service workshop for teachers in the use of multimedia teaching materials, particularly in French, which was his specialty; Matthew Hickey, a science teacher who had special interests in marine biology and urban ecology; Penny Bach, a young art teacher who had studied in Italy and was interested in the personal interrelationships of the fine arts, music, and literature; Ralph Kendricks, who compiled an anthology of black American writers; Anita Hackney, a social studies teacher who was born in the Panama Canal Zone and had served as a sponsor of Student Government programs in various Philadelphia schools; Dorice Wright, another social studies teacher who had previously taught as a Peace Corps volunteer in Tanzania, East Africa; and Mark Lyons, a graduate of the University of California who had spent a year in Atlanta working with high school dropouts in their anti-poverty program as well as serving a stint on the Program on Conscience and the Draft for the New York American Friends Service Committee.

A profile analysis of the experiential backgrounds of this well-integrated Parkway teaching staff showed that this group had already practiced their art in experimental and innovative educational programs. So, they were emotionally and academically ready to adjust to the challenges of the Parkway Program.

Many of the Parkway teachers had long hair and wore blue jeans and sandals to class. Because of the interns who flocked to the program, the student-faculty ratio became less than eight to one, and the average class size ran to fifteen, which was roughly half that of the regular Philadelphia high school's average class size.

The regular Parkway teaching staff was assisted by seven volunteer, senior intern students from Antioch College in Yellow Springs, Ohio, which had a long history of experimentation in its curriculum, particularly in its encouragement of work-study programs for its upper level students.

One of the Antioch interns liked his work as a tutorial teacher in his specialty of political science. "Our main job," he said, "is to help the kids order their own lives. Hardly anybody—including we teachers—is adequately equipped to handle freedom—and that is the heart of the matter."

The Parkway's "homeroom" teachers were also supplemented by various non-teachers from surrounding businesses, such as the Insurance Company of North America, the Bell Telephone Company, and the *Philadelphia Inquirer,* who doubled as part-time instructors when students came to visit their institutions on extended educational field trips.

At the Parkway, students are encouraged to participate in work-education programs, patterned after the successful Antioch college-level program. The benefits of this dual work-study curriculum are many. It means opportunities for social service for some, and for others it provides a means of clarifying their thinking about a future career when they graduate from school.

"The skills acquired in school should always be tested by something outside the educational system," Bremer argued in justifying this program. "If a student cannot do something—in an office, on a train, at the airport—somewhere, that he could not do before, it is highly doubtful that he has learned anything; it is certain that he has not learned anything useful." He incorporated this practical type of "reality-testing" so that the students could develop their own feedback system.

The students at the Parkway plan their own education with more freedom than is found in most traditional schools, subject to the specific minimum, state-required number of units in math, social studies, English, and language. Bremer believed that the students have to learn to be responsible for their own education and to make their own choices with the help of their teacher-counselors in the give-and-take of the tutorial groups. They have also helped to make the program's administration and organization part of the educational process. The students' practical suggestions made at the weekly town meetings have helped the administration to meet changing needs more readily.

Although most of the teachers at the Parkway believe that the students need to acquire certain intellectual virtues, they, along with Bremer, are not arrogant enough to set up such a "must list" of items that should be or ought to be learned at the moment.

Faculty offerings presently constitute roughly half of the courses of study available to the Parkway students. The other half is made up of courses taught by individuals and institutions in the community, which are recruited by Parkway students and teachers as interests in a given area are recognized; i.e., student interests in medically related professions led to the establishment of a series of paramedical personnel courses in several local hospitals; interest in stopping illegal voting procedures led to the director of the local Committee of Seventy (a group of civic-minded businessmen whose interest in good government extended to monitoring election frauds, etc.) and the start of a new course in election procedures; interest in journalism led to a series of internships with reporters at the local papers; interest in gemmology led to a special instruction class by a local jeweler; and interest in home economics led a group of mothers to organize a course in this area.

Parkway students have studied leathercraft, veterinary medicine, Swahili, and child psychology with the best specialists that the city can offer. If a student interested in cemetery management should join the program, there is little doubt that the Parkway officials would be able to find someone to help him.

Community professionals who volunteer their services as part-time instructors in these specialized courses are not paid, but are generally motivated to assume responsibility for the education of students out of an interest in the future of their own fields. These opportunities give the Parkway students a chance to sample a number of professions while still in high school instead of spending four years in one disciplinary area.

A student who has been "turned off" by the system for years may find his interest in academic subjects rekindled when he is given a second chance to study subjects previously denied to him.

The best testimony of the initial worth of the Parkway Program was that given by various students:

One chubby-faced, fourteen-year-old black student at the Parkway put it well when comparing his former public junior high

49

Discussion is important in the Parkway Program.

level place of learning with the new one. "In my old school," he confessed, "I was afraid to ask a question, because I thought the teacher would think it was stupid. Here I'm never afraid to speak my mind."

Another eleventh grade student commented that she welcomed the escape from the pressure which she experienced in her old school, the pressure to get good grades, where she had to put pressure on herself to excel. "But here you begin to realize that other things are more important, like answering questions: 'What am I doing?' or 'Why am I getting an education?' Here I feel I don't have to show anybody that I want to learn something. You don't have to apple-polish the teachers. Nobody else is responsible for my education but myself. It's up to me now."

After a Parkway Spanish-speaking class met at a building in the Puerto Rican, Spanish-speaking section of North Philadelphia, the students then left and walked around the neighborhood practicing what they had just learned by striking up conversations with passersby and local shopkeepers. One student who had failed his Spanish at his former school was amazed to discover how much easier it was to learn a foreign language at the Parkway where one had an opportunity to put his learning into immediate practice while it was still fresh in his mind.

A Parkway geometry class learned on the spot how to compute the diameter of a circle by going outside to test their skills by finding the true width of the beautiful Logan Circle with its mermaid fountain located in the center of the Parkway. This live experiential academic challenge beat a classroom paper and pencil math lesson of finding the diameter of a circle, as far as student motivation was concerned.

Besides academic-centered learning activities, the Parkway pupils are given many opportunities to exert leadership potential and good human relations. Management Groups at the Parkway are student organizations which help to run the program. When a specific problem is identified, the Management Group organizes itself to try to solve it. The purpose of this group is not only to involve the students in the administration of the Parkway Program in a serviceable way but to give them an opportunity for real leadership. Past Management Groups have become involved in areas of public relations, finding new space for classes, determining ways of improving communications within and between the three units of the Parkway complex, and discovering "who really has the *power* at the Parkway."

Although some groups have not been able to solve their immediate problems, their failures may be as educational as their successes, particularly if the students can identify the reasons for their failure and restructure their problems accordingly.

Closely allied to the Management Groups is the weekly town meeting, which functions as the House and Senate of the Parkway. At these periodic gripe sessions, an agenda is compiled that may run the gamut from how to obtain a water cooler to a discussion as to whether teachers should have a veto power over students. These meetings alternately provide lessons in group organization and group frustration. These "rap" sessions prevent morale problems from simmering for long, since plenty of opportunity is given to the students and faculty to air their views on a regular basis.

Some of the Parkway teachers had difficulty getting some of their students to attend the tutorial groups—the basic units of instruction which are held four times a week. Because students had the privilege of cutting these classes, it was often difficult to exert discipline. "Some of these kids just don't know how to handle freedom," commented one frustrated teacher. The one weapon that a Parkway teacher has at his disposal is the threat of withholding credit if he feels a student hasn't gotten enough out of a course.

In some cases, counseling with the disgruntled students would bring out the fact they were having trouble relating to a teacher or with other students. Once these misunderstandings were cleared up, they'd start going to class again. Bremer believed that the "tutorial is really a course in authority. Some teachers and students have mastered it, while others are still struggling with it. On a second level, it's learning to do a common task with a group of people you didn't choose to be with. On a third level, it's a basic social unit. It's a kind of home whether you want it or like it or not."

Bremer was cognizant of the fact that his first batch of students and teachers had all been "brainwashed" back in their old schools, and that it would obviously take some time to get them to adjust. But once they got over the first year's hurdle, he was convinced that things would settle down for a smoothly running operation.

Two students
visit a
local architect.

Some new faculty members have had some difficulty in adjusting to the new free-swinging atmosphere at the Parkway. When the Parkway's mini-skirted, blonde public relations representative, Lisa Strick, finished her first week at the program, she felt that she might never become accustomed to the casualness, chaos, and confusion there. She felt ready to climb the walls when she went to Bremer for some advice, asking him, "Is it always like this here?" The director answered: "Education is not a neat process. When you try to make it neat, it's not education." "I'll never forget what he said to me," commented Lisa.

The youthful Lisa also teaches a course in communications. She soon discovered that in order to steer a course between anarchy and too much structure, two things could be fatal. "One of these is saying to kids, 'You are going to shut up and do what I tell you,' and the other is 'What do you want to do?' " she said.

"I discovered that there are as many approaches as there are teachers, and eventually we achieved a state of mutual respect. I know more about the tools than they do, but they know what they want to do with them. They must cope with their society and they know ten times more about that than you do. If I just try to stick to my bag and be what I am, a white, middle-class liberal, I'm all right. But if I try to phony it up, they spot it right away," Lisa added.

Before the Parkway had completed its first semester, it had proved its general worth in many ways. Its chief sponsor, the Ford Foundation, appeared satisfied with its latest stepchild in the field of education.

By mid-1969, the Ford Foundation's education officer, Mario Fantini, said, "Up till now, we've had the notion that the classroom is the only place where learning can take place. The Parkway Program utterly rejects that notion; it breaks down the dichotomy between living and learning." [3]

As the end of the first semester approached, Bremer won a concession from his superiors to hold a lottery on June 13 to select 120 more students for a summer program. All of those lucky names that were drawn came from city high schools. Standing together on the John F. Kennedy Plaza near City Hall, 150 students (including most of the original 120 still at the Alpha

[3] Mario Fantini and G. Weinstein, *Toward a Contact Curriculum* (New York: Anti-Defamation League, 1967), p. 8.

Mrs. Lisa Strick, Director of Public Relations at the Parkway, instructing a class in journalism.

branch) helped Bremer select the names out of a large cardboard box marked "PP #2 Summer."

Bremer presided at the drawing, stating: "The whole city of Philadelphia is our campus and Philadelphia is our curriculum."

These students were to be assigned to the second, "Beta," branch of the Parkway. They started their studies in July while the rest of the regular public school students were enjoying their vacation.

The founding of the Parkway's second branch, Community "Beta," was the natural outgrowth of the expansionist needs of the Program and the cramped quarters at "Alpha." Because Bremer believed in sticking closely to his decentralized philosophy of small units of no more than 250 students, the birth of "Beta" had become a necessity by the end of the first (1969) spring semester of the Parkway Program.

To satisfy Bremer's new needs, the School Board signed a lease to acquire space in an old office building located at Twenty-third and Cherry Streets in a low-rent district within walking distance of the Parkway's cultural institutions. The Parkway Program had started to spread its wings.

A co-ed reading one of the many bulletin boards at the Beta Branch.

5. Gamma Becomes a Pseudonym for Paxson Parkway

"What educators must realize is that how they teach and how they act may be more important than what they teach."

Charles Silberman [1]

On June 20 an additional 360 students who were to start in the fall of 1969 at the third, "Gamma," branch were selected by random lottery from 2000 applicants. This group included parochial and suburban youngsters as well as Philadelphia public high school students.

The Parkway Program was by now organized into three basic decentralized branches, named after the first three letters of the classical Greek alphabet: *Alpha,* which still met for its homeroom, core activities in an old, abandoned bank building; *Beta,* which convened daily in its rented, two-story office building at Twenty-third and Cherry Streets, and *Gamma* which met in the condemned non-fire-resistant, former Paxson elementary school in North Philadelphia, at Sixth and Buttonwood, about a mile from the Parkway.

A strong believer in decentralization and the dangers of the curse of bigness, Bremer set out to keep the Parkway Program from becoming a bureaucratic monstrosity as it increased in size. By splitting his educational enterprise into three self-governing units, each with its own director, he made it possible for each unit to bring the students and faculty together for meaningful "town meeting" discussions where all could be heard.

John Bremer combined the best qualities of an accomplished

[1] Charles E. Silberman, *Crisis in the Classroom* (New York: Random House, Inc., 1970), p. 9, emphasis added.

showman and a dedicated philosopher. He was the right man at the right time to help launch this right idea in proper fashion. What he lacked in diplomacy, he made up in personal charm. He believed that by forging ahead, despite the abrasions of his personality on other school administrators, board members, or politicians, he was doing the right thing.

As a radical revolutionary, Bremer would not say it directly, but one could sense that, like his contemporary American educational iconoclast, Dr. Paul Goodman, the destruction of the old educational order and the building of a new one along the lines of his evolving philosophy were at the core of his plan. This underlying belief soon aroused the wrath of conservative members of the School Board, including Board President Richardson Dilworth, a former liberal, who gave Bremer a backhanded compliment by calling him a "genius."

Having not published any books of his own, and only a few articles, Bremer had to rely on outside mass-media trumpeters to spread the word of his exciting educational departures around the country. He made the best use of television and articles in the slick, mass circulation magazines to promote his ideas.

His flamboyance in grabbing headlines threw quite a few administrative noses out of joint, which chipped away at his effectiveness. But he kept doggedly onward in the pursuit of his goal to help make the Parkway Program a lasting and meaningful contribution to education and not to let it die as so many other innovative educational experiments had in the past.

In the ungraded Parkway classes, Bremer also made it possible for ninth grade students to be challenged more than when they were in an ordinary school by allowing them to mingle with high school seniors in their various twelfth-year-level curricular activities. (In the traditional high school, such mixing of grade levels was only possible in extracurricular or cocurricular activities, i.e., band, art, orchestra, glee club, and athletic teams.)

Although daily attendance is not compulsory, the percentage ratio of average daily attendance is higher at the Parkway than at the regular high schools in the Philadelphia system, where attendance at some of the more "difficult" schools regularly ran in the lower 70 percent level.

Informality and individual student responsibility are constantly emphasized at this institution. Students are allowed to smoke in

Two students contemplate
seminar on draft resistance.

class and call teachers by their first names if they wish. They are also not disciplined if they utter four-letter words, although the constant use of obscenities is not encouraged.

After getting settled down at the Gamma branch, a group of ten randomly selected high school students met one day in the abandoned Paxson elementary school on their lunch hour to discuss what America's most innovative and revolutionary school experiment—the Parkway Program—meant to them.

The six white and four black students all expressed personal enthusiasm for being lucky enough to be a part of this vital, pioneering educational experiment.

Colette, a sixteen-year-old transfer student from a fancy private school located on Philadelphia's Main Line, put it this way: "In my former, fashionable all-girls school, I felt cloistered and did not learn things that were relevant for this world." [2]

She was seconded by Donita, a fourteen-year-old black tenth grader, who also complained that her former public school "turned me off. Here we are one big happy family. There is no hostility. Everyone's together."

George, a long-haired, white seventeen-year-old six-footer, was vehement about why he was happy to be a part of the Parkway Program. "The public school has failed," he asserted. "We didn't get anything out of it. Learning was aimed at the wrong goals— like teaching us how many sheepherders there were in Kansas."

A seventeen-year-old Italian-American girl from South Philadelphia, Liz, compared her old school to the new one. "Our other schools were too big. We were just a number there at South Philly High with its 5000 students. Here we can be a person," she said proudly.

All of the seminar students waxed eloquent about how the Parkway Program differed from and surpassed their old school.

"We learn self-discipline here," said Donita. "You could waste a whole year here, but that is a rare occurrence."

"Yes," concurred Bob, a sixteen-year-old junior. "Many who had a 'goof-off' problem in their regular schools and had no sense of doing anything constructive feel a real sense of accomplishment here. There is no incentive to beat the Parkway system

[2] See my article, "School Without Walls," *Youth,* June 7, 1970, pp. 2-11. Many of these student comments are quoted in the article. Others are taken from hitherto unpublished notes.

because the educational system is not trying to beat us. We *are* the system."

"Back at our old schools," George countered, "the principal and counselors became irate and couldn't understand why anyone would want to leave their 'gorgeous' schools. They would try and keep us in the dark about what the Parkway Program was all about and how we could apply. But we found out; that's why we are here."

The thing that these turned-on students like the most about the Parkway is the attitude of the teachers.

"We have good communication with them [the teachers] here. Neither we nor they are under a strain," Donita chimed in.

Liz agreed: "The teachers are real people, not condescending. They exchange ideas with us on a more equal basis."

"That's because most of them are young and can identify with us," Colette observed.

"They were fed up with the old system that shackled them as well as us," George pointed out. "They don't go by the book in their teaching methods and what they do."

Because of this liberal, unrestrained atmosphere at the Parkway complex, the students feel that they learn more and are better motivated than their counterparts back at the regular schools.

"I like athletics," said seventeen-year-old Dennis, "especially the extra academic credit that I get here for being on the bowling team."

The enthusiastic and talkative Colette stressed that learning at the Parkway is a "two-way street," since it aids the teachers as well as the students. "Our written and oral evaluations are very important to us here, since we also tell the teachers what we think of them as well as listening to what they think about us."

"There is no danger of becoming a dull automaton here," asserted George, "since we are all treated equally. We can get more through cooperation than by competition, yet we still have chances to exhibit our own individualism."

The Parkway Program has also successfully bridged the generation gap between its faculty and student body. Many of the boys wear long hair with no chastisement from their elders or peers in the Program.

"When I'm walking down the street outside of the school," said George, "I have been stopped by truck drivers who ask me all the silly little questions and call me things like a 'fag.' One of them even chased me with a tire iron, but no one has ever called me a hippie. These adults have a lot of growing up to do at 45."

Donita laughed, "Some call us 'hippies,' but we don't mind."

"What's ironic about all this," said Ellen, another quiet senior student, "is that the old lady teachers and parents with blue-dyed hair, long bell-bottoms, and mascara have the nerve to try to tell us how to dress."

One of the more significant features that an outsider soon notes while visiting the Parkway Program is the lack of racial animosity in this well-integrated school.

"It is not there at all," said Bob proudly.

"Out there in the system," Dennis observed, "the school administration and the students are constantly at each others' throats. The government [high school administrators] doesn't want the students to have power."

"Here, student power is equal to faculty power. That's one reason why we also have racial understanding here, because no one is better than anyone else," George prompted.

Colette philosophized that "there is more respect here than at any other school in the city. Both we and the teachers learn to face facts."

"Right on," Bob said. "We can tell the teacher we hate him to his face, not behind his back, and he or she can take it and be a better teacher for it."

"There is complete freedom of speech here," agreed Donita, "and the teachers will tell you why they believe in it, if you ask them. Because they feel secure here for one thing."

On the matter of curriculum, the students felt that the Parkway had it all over their old schools.

"My course in the high school I went to before," commented George, "had me rostered into certain classes by a computer. Here, we have an integrated curriculum that is partly of our own choosing. We do not sit chained to the blackboard and chalk all day."

Bernadette, a black fifteen-year-old sophomore, spoke up for the first time. "You can pick your own course here that you can relate to. We are not square pegs being forced into round holes."

Most of them feel that the college student teacher interns from

A touch of humor in an integrated Parkway classroom.

Penn and Antioch, who are presently helping out the regular teachers at the Parkway, will be taking back the good ideas that they acquired during their stint at the complex to their new jobs and will probably try to infuse the old system with new ideas wherever they go in their careers.

"If a student is caught chewing gum in one of our classes," said one of the Parkway students with a chuckle, "the teacher here does not say 'Stop it!' but 'Do you have another piece?' "

Since Community Gamma is so far removed from the main Parkway cultural centers, most of the classes at the branch are held in the old Paxson school classrooms with the paint peeling off the walls, and graffiti everywhere. Because of a lack of usable school furniture, many of the students sprawl on the floor or on table tops in an informal atmosphere while classes are held. Many eat sandwiches or smoke while class is in session. They never fail to let their teacher know when he is assuming too much authority.

For example, in a class called "Socialist Realism," held at Gamma, a pupil had gone to the film library—at the teacher's suggestion—and found two films he thought the class should see. The boy said he wanted the class to see them the next week. But the teacher thought it would be better to wait until later in the term when the class would have a better idea what "Socialist Realism" is all about, and he started to assign reports to be given during the next few classes.

"That's not fair," said the boy. "You are only one person. If the class wants to see them next week, we go." Turning to the class, he asked, "Do you want to go?" The kids nodded their heads "yes." The teacher had been overruled.

The course dealt with the characteristics of socialist realism exhibited in Soviet literature, art, music, and film (art as propaganda). Students were allowed to take it for credit in English or social studies—whichever they needed.

The heart of the Parkway Program, however, was not found in the battered Alpha, Beta, and Gamma homerooms located near the majestic multilaned Benjamin Franklin thoroughfare, but rather could be found in the other learning locales that the students flocked to in the pursuit of knowledge. One of the less well-publicized institutions that quietly pitched in to help make the Parkway a success was the church. Although there was only one church located on the Parkway, the Roman Catholic Cathedral of Ss. Peter and Paul, over a dozen nearby churches and Jewish synagogues soon signified their willingness to cooperate with the Program by making their facilities available during the school day.

The Parkway Program was able to get around the traditional strictures of the separation of church and state in the matter of the use of church facilities, because it was not an example of a school run *by* a church but rather a school run *in* churches by public authorities. This important difference marked a significant breakthrough in the slow move toward a para-public school system in America, where the control of education rests with the public and not sectarian authorities.

The most important impact of the Parkway Program on the Center City churches, in the words of one cooperating minister, the Reverend Victor Carpenter of the nearby First Unitarian Church, is "its humanizing effect. The Parkway Program has been the chief reason why our doors are now unlocked from 9 to 5 daily," he said.

The neighboring conservative Protestant Swedenborgian Church also agreed to open its doors to Parkway students. This was a major move on their part since "they have never opened their doors for anybody else in twenty-five years," said one close observer of their congregation's activities.

Some of the Parkway students and teachers have made excellent use of Sunday school literature which they have found in various church classrooms, even though the denomination is not of their own choosing. This ecumenical rub-off on the students, faculty, and churches has had a positive effect. Parkway students read and profit by announcements of teenage church social activities and vice versa. Sometimes, with permission of the local minister, they will post announcements and even decorate the walls with colorful posters and art work of Parkway activities in which church members might be interested.

"They respond to their bulletin boards," said one religious education director of a leading Center City church. They particularly like to read *Colloquy* and *Youth* magazines which are interdenominational publications aimed at social problems of the teenage group, running from drugs to the draft.

One church experimented with a Parkway student acting as a liaison with his peers and school administrators after a tape recorder was found missing one day following a class in that particular church. The assignment of responsibility to see if the Parkway Program had any insurance to cover this loss and to help prevent the incident from repeating itself had a positive after-effect on the students.

Some of the Parkway students do tutorial work at several church day-care (Head Start) centers and give music lessons to the younger children (since there are always plenty of pianos available). Although most cooperating church Sunday school classrooms are used for English, math, and basic education, some of them have been utilized for sensitivity group training, song and dance classes, and art instruction.

During the pre-Christmas season a Parkway teacher wanted to show a film on a modern version of the Nativity of Christ to her mythology class. Since the Parkway has no audiovisual equipment of its own, she had to borrow a projector from a neighboring church, in this case the First Unitarian Church, where many Parkway classes are held. Her class of twelve students was fascinated with the film but was left somewhat confused. "It's fine—but how does it all end?" one of them asked.

The teacher was in a quandary until the religious education director of the church, Beth Ide, got an idea and loaned the teacher a record player and recording of the widely acclaimed, new English folk-rock cantata, *Jesus Christ: Superstar*. The playing of this musical selection helped most of her class to answer the question that had been plaguing them after viewing the film—the real meaning of Christ's birth, life, and death to high school students living in the late twentieth century.

6. The Death of a Dream

"A school is a prison that prepares you for the necessary nightmare."   *Jules Henry*

The original location of the Parkway's third branch, Community Gamma, was to have been the Spring Garden Institute on North Broad Street. This institution was centrally located and easy to get to by mass transportation, but by late summer the Board of Education decided that it was too expensive to rent this facility. So they switched their plans in early September and approved the reopening of the recently closed-down Paxson elementary school at Sixth and Buttonwood Streets. One hundred thirty randomly selected high school pupils were soon in attendance there.

Meanwhile, a series of events had taken place in another part of the city that would provide a supreme test for the whole Parkway philosophy and its ability to survive.

Back in the spring of 1969, a group of twenty-five elementary school parents in the Germantown and Mount Airy sections of Philadelphia withdrew twenty-four of their children from the local public schools during the last six weeks of the semester and put them into an underground "Basement School" taught by Caroline Snyder, an elementary school mother. These parents notified the superintendent and the School Board that they were seeking a meaningful alternative to the overcrowded "restraining and boring" public schools. They were informed by District No. 6 Superintendent, Dr. Bernard Kelner, that if they could find adequate space and the money to run their new enterprise, "they would get their dream."

Most of the parents agreed—in caucus—that if they could

67

attach themselves to one of the Parkway Program's three secondary branches, they would have their "dream." The only feasible location for their idea was the proposed Community Gamma. Dr. T. Richard Snyder, a Protestant urban missioner, who was one of the instigators of the project, his wife Caroline, and other parents met with Dr. Kelner and discussed the matter back in June, 1969. Following that meeting, Snyder had written Dilworth on August 22 concerning his group's desire to incorporate their novel idea into the public school system. "Can't we have a Parkway school, too?" he asked on behalf of the twenty-four other parents.

Dilworth replied on August 31 that he was leaving for a vacation and that their group would hear from Shedd shortly.

Shedd and Dilworth forwarded copies of the letters from Snyder to Bremer, who had already been thinking seriously about setting up a junior-sized version of the Parkway Program in combination with the Gamma branch. He believed that he had the support of his fellow educators in exploring the concept that if you ask older students to help younger ones, both would gain from the exchange of experiences.

After the Germantown parents had been told in late August that the Spring Garden Institute site had been rejected by the Board as a facility for the third Parkway branch, they ran an ad in the August 27 issue of the local Germantown *Courier* asking area parents if they were interested in an alternate school for their children.

Bremer, as a free-wheeling educator, worked under the assumption that the best way to cut through the bureaucratic red tape that permeates a big city school system, in order to get something worthwhile done, was to do it. This was the philosophical bent behind his decision to open a new elementary unit of the Parkway Program at the old Paxson Elementary School where the Gamma unit was located. This condemned gray-stone building stood as a lonely beacon surrounded by empty dirt lots, which had formerly contained factories and tenements in a ghetto redevelopment area of North Philadelphia.

Bremer's Paxson/Parkway experiment was based on his deep belief that "separating younger and older grades was artificial. The older children could help and be helped by the younger ones." When he got the official go-ahead in early September to

A Paxson/Parkway high school student counsels two elementary students.

use the old abandoned Paxson School for the programs, he felt it was too late to run a democratic lottery to select his elementary students. "I thought if we didn't get started, then we'd never be in the elementary business with the budget cuts coming just over the horizon."

He needed children desperately. "I had no kids," he said dejectedly. There were none in the immediate area because the Paxson School sits in the middle of the "bombed-out" East Callowhill Redevelopment Area and all of the old homes had either been condemned, boarded up, or leveled. Furthermore, this was the only school district in the city where the schools were not overcrowded.

Bremer knew where he could get a quick pool of students and he went after them. Up in Germantown, which was fast becoming a middle-class, black bourgeois section of the city, there was a surplus of students, whose concerned parents had already contacted him about doing something along the Parkway lines for the elementary level students.

Since Bremer knew that the school principals in Germantown would have little taste for his radical style of school reform, he turned to this group of parents, who were following up their newspaper ad with a telephone recruiting campaign to get the necessary number of children for his proposed Paxson/Parkway joint elementary and secondary school. "Those who were plugged into what was really going on got their kids in," remarked one mother.

On three occasions Bremer called Dr. Snyder to discuss the incorporation of the Basement School into the Paxson/Parkway plan. This group soon became the nucleus of the Paxson/Parkway elementary unit.

Dr. Shedd next called Snyder on September 4, giving them a go-ahead and agreeing to let them follow their general approach to the problem. On September 5, the interested Germantown parents met with Bremer to discuss ways of bussing their children to the alternative school site at Sixth and Buttonwood, some four miles from their area. Dr. Bremer assured them that he had the backing of both Shedd and Dilworth for his proposed joint elementary-high school branch of the Parkway.

The parents knew that time was now a factor. Within three days, they were able to recruit over one hundred willing parents who agreed to send ninety-seven of their children to the experimental school at Paxson. Dr. Snyder received a letter from Shedd stating that he knew what Bremer was doing and recommended that a 50-50 student population balance be attained, with half coming from the adjacent area around Paxson and the rest from Germantown.

Unfortunately, only nineteen students—all black—could be found in the East Callowhill area near the school; so the rest of the initial elementary student body—totaling some seventy-eight pupils—came from Germantown. Because 50 percent of this latter group was black, Shedd permitted the new elementary school to open for business on September 25.

When the Gamma branch opened at the old Paxson school in September, it was the only school in the community to have youngsters from kindergarten to the twelfth grade learning together under the same roof.

The transfers to Paxson were a jolt to the principals and parents of other youth in the schools involved, since most of them had no idea of what was going on. At the Henry School in West Mount Airy, for instance, where community groups had long been working to maintain a tenuous racial balance as well as a quality educational program at the school, twenty-one of the twenty-three youngsters who transferred were white. However, fourteen of the twenty-one who transferred from the Houston School were black. The transfers were viewed by many, though mistakenly, as indicating a lack of support by the School Board for maintaining these two sections of town as integrated communities. Fifty years ago, Germantown and Mount Airy were predominately white communities, but recently middle-class blacks have been moving into these sections in greater numbers.

What really happened was that two conflicting values clashed—that of a group of ethnically mixed parents who were interested in innovative reforms in education and that of another group interested in maintaining the stability of integrated education. Many other Germantown community residents complained that they had never heard of the Paxson/Parkway which added to their misunderstanding.

Dr. Shedd placed certain stipulations upon Bremer concerning the selection and bussing of elementary pupils to attend the Gamma unit. In a letter to Bremer dated October 21, 1969, the superintendent reiterated his conditions for his approving the continuance of the operation. They included informing and involving the district superintendent of the affected area and his school principals about the establishment of the complex and the selection of pupils; working out criteria for selection of the pupils with the district superintendent; and finally, a chance for the Board to express its views on the matter.

In order to protect himself, Shedd was adamant that while he agreed "in principle with the concept of an elementary and middle-school component of the Parkway Program, I did not make any commitments with regard to providing free transportation for students to the Paxson, or any other school, as part of this agreement."

This latter restraint did not deter the director of the Parkway Program, since he had assurances from the parents involved that they would set up their own car pools and personally foot the added transportation costs to get their primary-aged children into the program.

Dr. Shedd, on the other hand, was laying down the law to his maverick subordinate in order to clear up any "misunderstandings" and to "make absolutely certain that any previous commitments between us are perfectly clear."

The superintendent confessed privately to a sympathizer on November 3 that in "another month or two the Directorship of the Parkway Program would have to undergo a reappraisal since Dr. Bremer was unable to live with the political realities of the city." One of these realities was Bremer's bending of his own basic principles, under parental pressure, by allowing narrowly selected children into the new elementary branch, which caused many critics to sour on his whole program.

After the opening of the Paxson/Parkway School, some black parents in Germantown complained that the method of selection of students for the new complex was not democratic, that some white students had gotten in with "pull"; and so they brought pressure on the superintendent to do something about the situation.

Dr. Shedd, who came under extreme pressure from his own Board as well as from irate school principals and community groups in the wake of Bremer's actions, reluctantly decided that the best solution to what had become a confused and unhappy situation for all sides, was to close down the elementary unit at the Paxson School on December 19, 1969, even before the first semester was completed.

On November 24, the first bombshell fell on the struggling school when Dr. Shedd recommended at a televised School Board meeting the closing of the Paxson/Parkway on four grounds:

1. The undemocratic method of selection.

2. Economy (to supposedly save the school system some money, which his critics felt was a "red herring").

3. The effect on the racial balance of the Henry School (where twenty-one of the twenty-three pupils who transferred were white).

4. That Shedd and Dilworth did not know about Bremer's plans for the start of the new spin-off school-within-a-school. (Reliable informants have pointed out that Shedd reputedly sent Snyder a letter on September 2, which the latter never received. Bremer, however, received a courtesy carbon of the superintendent's letter agreeing with the Parkway director that he could open the elementary branch with his blessing.)

At the November Board meeting, Shedd denied openly that he knew about Bremer's plans, giving the impression that he never sent the original letter. The showdown in the power struggle between Shedd and Bremer had now come to a head faster than most observers had anticipated.

Meanwhile some three hundred Parkway secondary school students descended on the Board's meeting room on that evening of November 24 to protest the plans to drop the elementary branch of Paxson. Despite their appearance, Shedd held stubbornly to his position, since he knew that he had the Board's backing and both Shedd and the Board resented the pressure of public coercion.

Bremer defended himself on camera saying that he had Shedd's approval in the selection process for the Paxson/Parkway Program. Bremer publicly admitted that his selection plan was not the most desirable, pleading with the Board not to take it out on the children but on him, if they must have their pound of flesh. (The fact that almost one-third of the children came from the immediate area around Sixth and Buttonwood Streets, where the Paxson school stood, had no positive effect on the Board.)

When he made his announced decision to close the school before January 1, with the Board's backing, Shedd declared that if the Parkway administrator failed to notify the parents, then he would have to say that Bremer had been derelict. Shedd's ultimatum was in response to Bremer's last-minute plea that he remained "very hopeful" that the school would remain open beyond the forced closing deadline.

By Thanksgiving, Shedd believed that it was too late to reverse his private decision to close down the elementary branch of the Paxson/Parkway complex on the grounds that any other action would have caused a "serious reaction in District No. 6." (The superintendent of that district which included Germantown and Mount Airy, Dr. Kelner, had a reputation as a procrastinator. Kelner also had many friends and old colleagues on the school district's top administrative staff who brought pressure on Shedd on his behalf.)

Most of the parents were depressed by this recommendation by Shedd that the school be closed before it was even two months old. Mrs. Ella Mae Lipscomb, a black mother of an elementary child at the Paxson/Parkway, spoke from the heart when she described the impact of this new school on her child, just before its untimely closing. "It was done wrong, it was set up wrong," she said sorrowfully, "but as far as our black children are concerned, it is beautiful. My two children are thriving there beautifully. It would be a beautiful place for a child who is impatient, bored, and who feels that he isn't wanted.

"When my young son went to Paxson in September, he believed in Black Power, but now through his hustle and bustle, he has lost most of his arrogance and chip and he says to me, 'Mom, we all have to learn to live together.' I don't have no trouble with him now. The kids there don't feel the pressure. They feel they are being loved and wanted," said an appreciative Mrs. Lipscomb.

"I had even been taking my daughter, Levita, to three different hospitals while she was attending the old school because they said she was 'hard of hearing.' But now I have found out that wasn't her trouble at all. She was just 'going into a shell' back there and turning herself off and not listening. Now she is coming out of her shell and I am grateful," said the twenty-eight-year-old mother of three.

During another publicly televised School Board meeting held two weeks later on December 8, several parents of Paxson/Parkway elementary students testified that their children individually and collectively did much better at the new school than at the old. Many of the pupils who had been labeled "underachievers" in their former schools were better motivated and improved their reading abilities in the new atmosphere.

One parent of a second grader described how his black child had fought with a white classmate, but a week later they were working together harmoniously making puppets of a black girl and a white girl fighting one another. They took out their "racial animosities and hostilities through playacting," said the parents.

Another parent pointed out that the children really did not leave their other schools to go to the physically older, but educationally newer Paxson school, "since they were not really a part of the old system in the first place."

"Please don't punish our children for the mistake of Dr. Bremer in his selection process," pleaded one parent. "If you must punish Bremer, do so, but not our kids!"

If Bremer had been hasty in selection plans, the Board compounded his error with an equally hasty decision to bury a healthy idea whose time had come.

Some observers felt that Bremer might win the battle and lose the war by creating a public fuss, thus forcing the Board and Shedd to reverse themselves. Dr. Shedd and the Board's solution to the furor was to take a stern, sweeping-the-problem-under-the-rug attitude of "Let's not try to solve the Paxson/Parkway—let's close it."

Dr. Bremer did not help his cause when he admitted that he was in an irrepressible hurry to open the new grade school unit. He had moved ahead without having obtained the full support of his superiors. *The Evening Bulletin* (Philadelphia) castigated him for his actions in a December 1, 1969, editorial when it opined: "He [Bremer] may now be reflecting that undue haste is a poor basis on which to win community support for his innovative style of schooling."

The issue simmered for another two weeks and the Board decided that one more public hearing was needed before Christmas. So at another televised Board meeting held on the evening of December 22, more than one hundred citizens came to the school district auditorium prepared to testify against the closing of the Paxson/Parkway elementary school in a last-ditch effort to save their school. Three parents of Paxson students took up most of the Board's regular meeting which lasted one hour and ten minutes; so President Dilworth had to adjourn the main meeting and split his Board up into three panels to accommodate the 101 remaining witnesses who wished to be heard on the subject.

He was annoyed at the deluge of protests, calling them "slick tactics." "I don't think it is slick tactics," said one irritated Paxson parent, whereupon Dilworth cut in and shouted: "It is slick tactics, and you know it doggone well!"

After that outburst, the Board agreed to hear only three more couples on the subject, out of twenty-five who were on the waiting list to testify. The thrust of the protesting parents' testimony was a request to the Board to keep the elementary branch open until June to give it a real test before they arbitrarily closed it down. But the Board would have none of this compromise plan and stubbornly refused to alter its earlier decision.

Dr. Snyder, who came to the speaker's stand with his wife, referred to the decision to close the Paxson/Parkway school by declaring: "The only thing our children have learned is not to trust the school district. The blacks have known that all along." He concluded that the closing of the school appeared to be "an arbitrary and capricious decision resulting from an administrative error."

Ironically enough, the Advisory Committee for the Parkway Program, consisting of Cliff Brenner; John Patterson, former head of the Educational Task Forces for the Dilworth Board; Joel Bloom, Director of Science Education at the Franklin Institute; and Dr. Bernard Watson, Deputy Superintendent of Schools for Planning, was used only once during Bremer's tenure. That single consultation occurred during the Paxson/Parkway crisis at the tail end of 1969 when Dr. Bremer tried to get this committee to support him in a last-ditch effort to save the program.

He failed in his endeavor and the Paxson concept went under. In the behind-the-scenes battle over this issue, Cliff Brenner saved Dr. Bremer from actually being fired on the spot by the Board. (This fact was not made known at the time when newspaper headlines were chronicling the daily blow-by-blow accounts of the struggle between Bremer and the School Board.)

One School Board member, Mrs. Ruth Bennett, confessed later that "Shedd also got himself boxed into a corner by his adamant insistence to close down the elementary branch of the Paxson/

Parkway, when the majority of our board was ready quietly to reverse themselves and keep it open. He refused to budge and we almost fired him over that issue."

But Dilworth stuck with Shedd and helped him to save face and his job.

In a personal interview Robert Blackburn, the Deputy Director of the Office of Intergroup Education at the school district headquarters, summed up the dilemma facing the principals in the case by observing that "there was an intricate, symbolic issue at stake in the Paxson/Parkway experiment. When the black-run *Philadelphia Tribune* ran a series of articles condemning the so-called racial discrimination at the new branch, Shedd was advised by the black leaders to 'cool it' and not to punish Bremer.

"The parents involved left themselves vulnerable, however," commented Blackburn (who is now deputy superintendent in Oakland, California). "The fact that both Shedd and Bremer are prima donnas added to the conflagration."

Blackburn added that Bremer had hurt himself in this struggle by his contempt for the other principals which caused them to withdraw their support in the crunch.

Dr. Shedd moved very fast to cover the stain that started to spread over the entire Parkway Program. He claimed that his step to eliminate the elementary setup at Paxson saved the secondary level Parkway Program from the critics.

Betty Barth, the Administrative Assistant at Community Gamma, felt disillusioned with Dr. Shedd's explanations for the closing of the Paxson/Parkway elementary branch. "His reasons were inadequate and almost irrelevant in the eyes of the thousands of regional TV viewers," she lamented, even though the rest of the city backed him up in his decision.

On January 7, 1970, after the furor over the closing began to die down, Shedd sent a rationalizing, follow-up letter to Cy Schwartz, the Unit Head of the Gamma branch. It read in part: "This recommendation to close the elementary branch should not be construed as a criticism of the program at the Paxson/Parkway school. Nor does it mean that this school system is turning its back on alternatives to the more traditional forms of education. In fact, for the next school year, the Board has indicated its willingness to consider recommendations regarding the establishment of Parkway type programs within those districts whose communities express a strong desire to have, and a commitment toward, the kind of education that can be obtained through such a program.

"Until such times as we are able to move forward again in this and in many other areas, my recommendation to the Board will have to remain as it now stands."

One Paxson/Parkway parent felt that the real reason for the closing of the school was not racial. "Rather it was an irrational motivation on Shedd's and the Board's part, since neither of them received credit for the birth of our school and missed the psychological response that one gets from fathering a new concept that gets a lot of good publicity. The Board's ire was aroused because it was not their idea. All their other arguments were merely a 'put-on.'"

While it was operational, however, the Paxson/Parkway elementary branch gave the high school students and their teachers an opportunity to bridge the gulf between the two major age groupings of learning.

"It was beautiful to have the little kids here," wistfully commented George, a Gamma branch senior student at Paxson. "I had a third grade friend who knew me. He came out of his shell."

Liz agreed: "They taught us, since they adapted to this new system of learning faster than we did. They were more flexible."

"We high school students in the program got more enjoyment out of our learning as we tutored them," said Donita.

"We got a feeling that we were helping to prepare them for the future," volunteered Thelma, sixteen, one of the quieter students present.

"We all got a good feeling," Bob interrupted. "For many, it was the first time they were helped in their lives. We were more together during the closing of the Paxson/Parkway experiment than at any other time in our lives." [1] Many of these [Community Gamma] high school students testified at the televised School Board meeting for two weeks in succession during December, 1969, when the question of the future of this stepchild of their program was being debated by school officials. It was their first taste of being part of the political process and although they lost the battle—with the closing of the elementary branch of the

[1] Adapted from Donald Cox, "School Without Walls," *Youth*, June 7, 1970, p. 10.

78

Parkway Program—they, in a sense, won the war, since they had achieved a great deal of public sympathy and civic pride for their cause.

In the aftermath of the tragic and premature closing of the Paxson/Parkway school, parents of fifty-four of the children got together and decided to form a private school to tutor their children rather than send them back to their original public schools. The leaders of the new alternative were again Dr. Snyder and his wife Caroline, the parents of a five-year-old who attended Paxson. Snyder served as the chief spokesman for the new group, which sent applications for private tutoring to the Pennsylvania State Department of Public Instruction.

A state school board official reluctantly agreed to process the applications, despite the fact that not all of the proposed teaching-tutorial staff were certified. The new alumni offshoot of the former Paxson/Parkway educational experiment was dubbed "Project Learn" by its founders.* Temporary housing was found in a little used Sunday school building located behind the Germantown Unitarian Church. The setting was ideal, since it was located in a miniature forest grove of tall oaks surrounded by azaleas.

Snyder, who was Director of Theological Studies for the Metropolitan Associates of Philadelphia, an urban research and action organization, announced that tuition would average $35 per month, per pupil, for those who could afford to pay it. Teachers either volunteered or worked on half-salary.*

Just before the final debacle of the Paxson/Parkway school, Bremer even tried to mount a quiet campaign for himself to replace Shedd as school superintendent. But this semi-subversive and ill-starred attempt to undermine Shedd did not sit well with either the superintendent or the Board and hurt Bremer badly as a professional educator. In English parlance, his infighting against his boss wasn't "quite cricket."

Dr. Bremer later claimed that his new Paxson/Parkway unit was sabotaged before it really had a chance to prove itself. By late 1970, Shedd preferred to let the whole issue die with this parting observation: "The Paxson/Parkway concept was six months premature."

---

* See Chapter 12.

7. The First Commencement on the Grand Staircase

"At a time when other schools are experiencing disruption, it is heartening to witness what the Parkway has achieved."

Dr. James E. Allen [1]

By early 1970, other cities were taking an active interest in the Parkway Program. Daily delegations of dozens of local school administrators kept flocking to Philadelphia from all over the nation to observe the program firsthand. Two large cities, Chicago and Milwaukee, were the first to take the plunge and establish a small pilot Parkway-type program of their own. Hartford, Washington, D.C., San Francisco, and Kansas City were also thinking of following suit in short order.

As the first anniversary of the Parkway Program approached, John Matthews of the *Washington Star,* January 30, 1970, termed the project as "the most exciting and perhaps the most significant thing going on today in American education," after a visit to the complex. His rosy assessment was shared by other observers who came to look over this controversial phenomenon.

Bremer was confident that the next year would be less rocky than the first. "We've won the war in a year," he said. "We now have too large a political base in the community to be destroyed." His feeling was based on the belief that even though he had lost an arm in the battle of the Paxson/Parkway, the main body was still intact.

"Our program has a constituency because it's an educational program. Our aim was not to set up a political power base first,"

[1] From a speech by James E. Allen, then U.S. Commissioner of Education, at first Parkway commencement, February 17, 1970.

he said. "We are a public institution and that's damn important. Our aim was to produce first an educational program that because of its very nature would command political support, and that's what we have accomplished."

Bremer discussed his first year's trials at the Parkway School before a local Chamber of Commerce winter conference in January, 1970. In his somewhat acid remarks, the director of the school without walls pointed out that there was little chance for a learning environment to exist in either the schools or the city when there was no interaction between them. He challenged his listeners from the local power structure with a reminder that "learning is the process by which our city renews herself . . . so that we can in a sense fall in love with her again . . . because she is the source, the major source, of beauty in our lives. Now this means that the city changes, and it is by changing that she preserves herself as a matrix of all that is good in human life." [2]

Although he had remained relatively apolitical during his short stay in Philadelphia, Bremer put his finger on one of the sore spots in the community—the knowledge that the current incumbent of City Hall, the Democratic Mayor James H. J. Tate, was serving out the last two lame duck years of a ten-year reign. This atmosphere was mirrored in Bremer's words: "How weary, stale, flat, and (if I may be forgiven) unprofitable seems the reality of a city kept like the fossil bones of a once potent creature as a reminder of how great we used to be.

"How unjust and inhuman our lives can be in Penn's fair city that once sustained and nourished the tradition of civility! How oppressive and degrading human life can be, in a city dedicated to the rule of law! And how easily we tolerate educational disaster in a city that boasts the founding of the first public school in the original thirteen colonies!"

Bremer's philosophy after a year of operations at the Parkway could be summarized as follows:

"Don't categorize, classify, judge, or evaluate students by putting them into boxes. This only creates competitive situations that often lead to students fighting among themselves.

"We should be teaching cooperation not competition.

"We should have a self-reflecting student body where the learning community is always kept small (with a maximum size of 150

[2] *The Sunday Bulletin Magazine* (Philadelphia), Feb. 22, 1970. p. 1.

students). This is to make it possible that no one feels that he is a small fish in a large pond, thus making the school more livable.

"We don't have decent education in the suburbs because the students there invest more of their energies fighting fear and guilt brought about by their isolation from the problems of the neighboring cities and curricula built around white-oriented studies.

"Where the level of student anxiety and hostility has been reduced (as we have tried to accomplish at the Parkway), the drug and smoking problems become almost nonexistent."

In less than three years, the unique Parkway Program had come a long way from an amorphous idea as a viable alternative for a new multimillion dollar high school that might have taken up to ten years to complete. As its first anniversary approached, it was not only operational, but ready to graduate its first senior class of eight students.

The graduation, held at noon, Tuesday, February 17, 1970, was something between a Hollywood production and a Quaker meeting. Since it marked the first anniversary of the Program, the grand staircase of Philadelphia's famed Art Museum at the head of the Parkway served as the stage. Bremer was shrewd enough to invite the press, radio, and TV stations to cover the affair and to set up their floodlights and cameras. This mass-media coverage gave the struggling Parkway Program an extra boost. The students sprawled all over the main staircase while their parents and V.I.P. guests sat on the marble floor at the foot of the steps.

In opening the informal ceremonies, the boyish and jolly Bremer made a sarcastic introduction, saying, "I don't get a chance to make public statements anymore; so I'm going to make some remarks." Everyone in the audience knew that he was getting back at Superintendent Shedd and the Board for gagging him following the recent demise of the Paxson/Parkway.

In his opening remarks, Bremer repeated his guiding philosophy that the Parkway Program has demonstrated: "There are a million ways to learn, a million ways to teach. Those who say that 'this is the way'; 'this is the orthodoxy' are bound to fail. . . ."

To those who wondered if there was sufficient orderliness in the program, Bremer had a word: "It is clear that there is no learning without order. We are not unstructured. We are merely structured differently.

"On the other hand, there is no learning without disorder, a disorder in which the student is involved in ordering," he concluded.

The main speaker at this "mini" commencement was Dr. James E. Allen, then the U.S. Commissioner of Education, who told the students and their parents that he was impressed with "the enthusiasm and commitment to change in education" on the part of the faculty and students in the Program. "We in the U.S. Office of Education are watching this program with interest," he said.

"I felt back in the fall of 1969 that the hope for change in our schools lay with the students. The significant thing here," he said, "is that while other cities are still talking about reforms in education, they are a reality here at the Parkway." Allen then ticked off the unique characteristics of the Parkway Program, i.e., the tutorial program, the new system of evaluating students and learning experiences, and the "recognition that educational opportunities lay beyond the school and in the community."

Achieving such a goal is not easy, he pointed out. "As far back as 1916, educators talked about getting into the community, but few took the plunge. Today more and more people are now recognizing that the human element is still the most important one in education, and I think this concept is linked to the spirit of Philadelphia," he said.

"At a time when other schools are experiencing disruption, it is heartening to witness what the Parkway has achieved," he told the eight hundred Parkway pupils and guests. "To many observers, this young program is the most exciting and probably the most significant innovation going on in American education today."

At the conclusion of his Parkway commencement address, Dr. Allen said that he hoped the ideas, spirit, and success of this unique educational program might soon spread through the nation in the same fashion as the fervor for independence that emanated from Philadelphia two hundred years ago as a result of the vision and zeal of our founding fathers. This could be the prime legacy of the Parkway Program in the turbulent seventies.

Bremer did not miss a chance to get in some barbs at the school administration with his set of brief remarks following Allen's speech. In his prescription for the future of the program, he noted the need to expand the program based on the tremendous student demand (10,000 applications in June, 1969 alone). "We ought to go back into the elementary school business as soon as possible," he stated, a remark aimed at Shedd and the School Board in the wake of their closing of the Paxson/Parkway two months before.

"We need to set up a nongeographical school district, to educate children no matter where they live," he went on.

"It is only a question of time before the students get more deeply into the governing of the program, when they will see for themselves the problems of forcing public action.

"Finally, we have had inquiries already of student exchange from all over the United States, Canada, England, and even California—to send students here."

The exuberance of the students and parents was exhibited at the graduation when the first graduate marched up to get his diploma, wearing a white Edwardian mod suit, covering a shocking pink shirt with ruffles at the wrists, and sporting a long, Beatle-length hairdo. Some of the girls wore micro-miniskirts and even the staff got into the act by congratulating the female graduates with a kiss on the cheek instead of a formal stiff handshake.

The eight graduates who received their diplomas from Bremer and Allen were typical of the freedom of dress that characterized the Parkway Program. One boy even wore a sweater. When the last graduate went by the receiving line, she received a kiss on the cheek from the guest of honor, Dr. Allen.

After Allen's speech, Bremer pulled another radical departure from the norm of traditional high-school commencement ceremonies. In the spirit of an old-time Quaker meeting, he asked for live testimonials from parents, faculty, students, or anyone who cared to share a thought about the program. One mother got up, and with tears in her eyes, thanked the school for bringing her son out of his shell. "You saved his life," she said.

A teacher reported that he'd been personally turned-on by the program. He said, "No one thinks of *teachers* who drop out of the system, but they do, either literally or figuratively, just like students." One of the undergraduate students, halfway up the steps, arose and said: "I just want to say that Parkway is a wonderful loving thing. Every one loves each other."

There was one shadow cast over the otherwise happy proceedings, however. Only one School Board member out of nine showed up for this historic occasion. Significantly, he was the youngest member of the Board, George Hutt, a black. Most of Shedd's top administrative staff also boycotted the festivities, although the

84

place of graduation was only a short walk, a few blocks from their offices down the Parkway.

Significantly, too, Dr. Shedd was conspicuous by his absence from this historic gathering, as was School Board President Dilworth, which was a mark of the strained relations between these two key educators and Bremer. (Shedd was vacationing with his wife at Miami Beach, but he could have been at the graduation if he had really wanted to be there.)

The benediction at the first graduation was given by an undergraduate Parkway student instead of the usual minister, priest, or rabbi. A long-haired student stood up and with tears in his eyes said, "All things are beautiful. We are all beautiful!" and then he sat down.

The first commencement at the Parkway was over.

8. The Decline and Fall of J.B.

"How weary, stale, flat, and (if I may be forgiven) unprofitable seems the reality of a city kept like the fossil bones of a once potent creature as a reminder of how great we used to be."

Dr. John Bremer

When the Parkway Program was just over a year old, *Time* magazine, of March 23, 1970, was saying: "The most interesting high school in the U.S. today does not have a classroom it can call its own. But every week, some 30 to 40 school administrators come to Philadelphia to examine the Parkway Program high school."

By this time, Bremer felt that he had carried the Parkway Program beyond the experimental state. "I think we've not only proved ourselves," he said confidently, "but proved the necessity of providing alternate forms of education within the public school system. We're no longer a model that will work for a semester, or a year, or two years. I think we are here to stay."

He stubbornly clung to his messianic belief that his program was a welcome relief from the traditional urban public school straitjacket that he called a "disaster area"—where children are channeled for four years into programmed, 42-minute-long classes that usually lead to boredom, apathy, and rebellion.

Bremer was not content to rest on his original limited curriculum but briskly set about to expand the program far beyond its early blueprints. He soon established an auto-mechanics class in a nearby auto-repair shop, a leather-working class in a leather shop, a journalism course in the offices of the Philadelphia *Evening Bulletin,* and dozens of others taught on location. This sounded much like a pattern similar to the old European guild system whereby the trades and handicrafts were taught, in the post-Middle Age era, to apprentices by a master craftsman on the job rather than in a vocational school.

There were differences, however, from this old-fashioned guild training concept as practiced in days of yore. While the guild system was restricted entirely to blue-collar type, skilled artisan trades, the Parkway experiment was centered around both semi-skilled and specialized skills courses taught by professionals. Unlike a modern vocational school, which was the successor to the guild system, the Parkway aimed more at educating students for white-collar, public service type careers as well as preparation for college.

For instance, a physician gives a course in health services, a jeweler in gem cutting, and an art historian gives a course in art history. As an integrated comprehensive school, the Parkway has not ruled out the so-called blue-collar careers, and so one finds a printing course taught by a union printer along with secretarial sciences, color photography, and other similar courses for those who are desirous of specializing in any other particular fields of endeavor.

In addition to these special, vocation-oriented course offerings more sophisticated courses began to appear in the general education area. Such new courses as "Famous American Riots," "My Country, Right or Wrong?", "How a Baby Develops," "Paramedical Services," "Oriental Religions," "Happenings," "Model Rocketry," and "Filmmaking" were introduced into the expanding Parkway Program curriculum.

By March, 1970, the second-year catalog of the Parkway bulged with some 250 course offerings as Philadelphia's burgeoning downtown area literally and figuratively became the Program's main campus, with students making their way from class to class by foot, subway, bike, or bus.

As Earth Day approached in the early spring of 1970 (April 22), the Gamma branch of the Parkway offered a course on "The Woods," built around the ecology of nature and the interrelationship of plants, trees, and animals. The ease with which curriculum change can take place in a program like the Parkway to adjust for fast-changing events like the rise of the ecology movement is one of its prime assets as compared with the more rigid

A Parkway student studying the growth
of a human fetus at Biology Museum,
University of Pennsylvania.

curriculum offerings of the traditional public schools which are programmed years, and sometimes decades, in advance.

Some students miss the athletic activity that marked their old school ties. Although there are still no school sports, band, orchestra, cheerleaders, or the usual other extracurricular activities at the Parkway, the students make up for this "loss" by integrating the old concept of the usual after-school cocurricular activities into the daily curriculum pattern.

In the second year of the program, however, some of the students gradually became somewhat disillusioned when they couldn't get through to Bremer for advice as they had during the first crucial year. Many students felt Bremer was losing faith in the effort when he would so often tell them curtly to go to their unit head, or when he didn't show up at Town Meetings as he had earlier. What they didn't understand was that Bremer deeply felt that he had to withdraw eventually from such daily contacts if the program was to succeed. They would all have to learn to work without him as a "father figure."

Bremer firmly believed that the task of the educator was to create a matrix which would support everyone who wanted to be in it, but that he must also prevent any one individual from capturing complete control of it. That meant Bremer, too.

The informal atmosphere of the program was typified by the fact that on the bulletin board in Community Gamma there were announcements about several different matters not directly related to the school, including a telephone number to call for birth control information.

Free-wheeling graffiti is in evidence everywhere at Gamma—and not just in the rest rooms. Some of the graffiti on the walls of Parkway facilities really are far out. One of them wistfully shows a palm tree and a thatched hut on a desert island with this slogan underneath: GET AWAY FROM POLLUTION.

Another one had inscribed inside the peace symbol: ALL YOU NEED IS PEACE. Many teachers encourage such student graffiti on the grounds that it encourages creative expression. "It also helps them to occupy their free time constructively," observed one teacher, "and it keeps them out of trouble."

The director of Gamma isn't happy with the homespun graffiti; so he encourages his students to do creative "stuff" like psychedelic murals instead.

A student painting an original mural-graffiti on classroom wall while fellow student watches.

When it was discovered that visitors from another school had left their names and other graffiti on the peeling hallway walls in their Community Alpha bank loft, Bremer called in a fund-raising management group of students. The next thing he knew, some students were conducting a cake sale at the corner of Eighteenth and Market Streets, and they raised over $60 to buy paint to re-decorate the walls properly.

Bernie Ivens, a bearded math teacher who wears sandals and blue jeans to class and who prefers instructing in the informal atmosphere of the Paxson (Gamma) branch, has a special knack of bringing his class along with him with a rare sense of grace and good humor that often brings applause from his class when he finishes. A veteran of eight years of teaching at West Philadel-phia High, Ivens explained in a personal interview why he volun-teered to take the gamble with Bremer's dream. "The Parkway philosophy was consistent with my own—that the students and teachers can work cooperatively with the administration," he said. "I thought maybe the whole idea was a fake, but I soon found out it was for real. Now it's a joy for me."

"I'm sure uptight teachers wouldn't be happy here. It's not like a jailhouse where you have to be the keeper of thirty-five kids. Everyone is trying to help each other out. The old system, with its strictures like bells and set periods, seems so ridiculous to me now as I look back. Here you know the kids well. The kids think nothing of calling you up and coming over to your home to see you for help. I don't see how it's possible for them *not* to learn. In my classes at the Parkway, I'm covering more material and covering it faster."

In Ivens' advanced class at the Gamma branch, he was free to give individual tutorial help after passing out some mimeo-graphed work sheets to the whole class. Following a 10-minute session for homeroom announcements, one student, a girl in blue jeans, didn't go along with the rest of the class who were con-centrating on the assignment. She quietly read the latest issue of *Liberation,* an underground newspaper, instead. Unlike the typical public school, no one bothered her or called her to task for this seeming "insubordination."

Occasionally, the quiet of the class was broken when a student shouted with exasperation over some frustrating stumbling block that prevented him from solving the problem before him. The predominantly silent atmosphere reflected the concentrated individual work that was taking place in the room.

The Parkway Program showed among other things that learning could be fun. On one sunny spring day in 1970, a group of playful Parkway students at Gamma threw a couple of worn sofa cushions out a third-floor classroom window of the Paxson school. They narrowly missed hitting a woman passerby on the head. An irate man, who observed the incident, came storming into the office to report the altercation, and he demanded that the students be disciplined. Two of the students involved went down to the street, retrieved the cushions whose stuffing poked through the covers, and brought them back inside. That was the sum total of their punishment at the Parkway.

At another public school, they probably would have been reprimanded, suspended, or given some more severe form of disciplinary action. (Fortunately, no one was hurt and the incident did not repeat itself.)

The recent classroom showing of a filmed rerun of a CBS Documentary Report on "Conformity," narrated by Harry Reasoner, provided the motivation for a lively discussion, the role of the individual and the group, by a class of senior Parkway students. This film was written and produced a few years ago by Reasoner's son.

When the teachers suggested that the students move up front after the completion of the film to discuss it, many of them rebelled and said they would stay in the back of the room. "We are individualists," they said defiantly, but with a sense of humor.

Another one shouted: "I am conforming with my peers; that's why I wear long hair," in response to a summary question by the teacher on what the film was all about.

One student's comment on the film reflected the free spirit of the typical Parkway student: "The public school kids in the film all looked like a bunch of zombies. They all stood up together. They don't question the words in the textbook. The teacher is always right and if you're ever found wandering in the halls, you'd better get to your classes pronto—or else."

Most of the class felt that the majority's urge to conform, as depicted in the film, still exists today, but in a slightly different form, as far as public school students are concerned. "Most just do not want to risk rebellion," one girl said.

Ed Fruit, the teacher, commented: "Conformity isn't necessarily a dirty word, since standards and mores are different today. At the Parkway there is less conformity because we try to teach you as individuals. When you get to college, you will hopefully be more mature and have a one-upmanship jump over the public school graduates."

Meanwhile, all was not serene at the top administrative levels of the Parkway Program. The Philadelphia School Board refused to accept the new $300,000 foundation grant to help the embattled Parkway Program in early 1970. Their rationale was based on the increasing pressure from City Hall, particularly from the City Council president and the mayor who were vehemently opposed to expanding the program and didn't appreciate its innovative outcomes.

By early spring, 1970, when the annual school budget planning time arrived, the City Council president began to criticize the Parkway Program in press conferences. He charged that the money spent on the Program benefited only a few students out of the thousands in the Philadelphia schools.

Later in the spring, the council president again attacked the Parkway Program charging that its experimental program disturbed people, particularly at a time when the school system was under great financial pressure. Board President Dilworth defended the Parkway Program, pointing out that in a time of change, innovation and experimentation were vital necessities in the light of the obvious deficiencies of the existing educational system. He also noted that the Program consumed only a relatively small portion of the total school budget.

At a School Board meeting in early June, 1970, a group of anxious parents challenged the Board about the future of the Parkway Program. A new coalition of parents, teachers, students, and community representatives got together and spoke of their anxieties concerning the moribund situation.

"While you fail to act, we are acting," said one Parkway parent. "We want to work with you, but that requires cooperation. Are you ready to work with us? We want an answer! We also expect answers, and dialogue, on other specific questions . . . because the program's leadership has been threatened. Our coalition has taken steps to consider appropriate alternatives."

She demanded to know the School Board plans concerning the

proposed expansion of the Project and asked for a public policy stand on the matter.

Shedd gave a qualified answer to her questions, stating that the Board had met earlier in the day with Bremer (in the Executive Board meeting where the "real" decisions are made away from the public eye). "We exchanged viewpoints (a diplomatic substitute for the word "clash")," said the superintendent, "and agreed to end the freeze on applications for potential students for next year."

"There are no provisions to expand the Program on any basis at this time," he said, noting that only enough new applications would go out that month to fill the eighty vacancies created by graduating seniors. He hoped, however, that Board action on expanding the Program would come soon, but gave no hint of a date.

In the closed Board meeting held earlier in the day, Bremer learned that his bosses were still trying to work out the form of a proposal that would satisfy the Ford Foundation so that the city could get another $294,000 grant for further development of the Parkway effort. Bremer had written a plan that would provide for faculty training and expansion into the elementary- and middle-school levels to bring the total Parkway enrollment up to 900. This plan would encompass a nongeographic, programmatic, model-school district with its attendant evaluation.

The Board countered Bremer's proposal with one of their own, backed by Shedd, to transform the entire Parkway Program into a junior year (eleventh grade) effort only, which Bremer called "insipid . . . educationally unsound and administratively impossible." This dilemma of continuing hassles with the Board put Bremer in an almost impossible bind with his superiors. He let the Board know, however, that he had had good offers from several other school systems and had about reached the point where he felt he would be getting "in the way" if he stayed on at the current level of expansion.[1]

A few days later, he told a committee of the Parkway community, which had been set up to find a possible successor, that he did not necessarily want to leave, but would not be able to "hang around" if other cities sought him out with his ideas. He en-

[1] This and subsequent statements by Bremer were quoted in John Zeh, "Will School Board Let Parkway Suffocate?" *Distant Drummer,* June 11, 1970, p. 3.

94

couraged the committee not to let the program remain directorless, if he should leave, or have someone undesirable (new leader) forced upon them.

He warned them to watch out for Shedd and the Board. "Make sure that in the future you keep control of the Program so someone can't knock it out or change it," he told the coalition confidentially.

Bremer also insisted that the entire community should have a greater role in directing the Parkway in the future. "We should be moving toward having students, staff, and parents taking a more active political role to make sure we use the program's design to the fullest," he said. "Their role has got to change. You've got to keep tabs on the new man or he will turn [the program] into a school. Whether I go or stay, I feel the relationship between the director and students, parents, and staff ought to be different than I've had." [2]

Because of the delicate financial condition of the rest of the school system, the School Board could no longer afford to have a maverick rocking the boat in the Parkway swells while they were trying to obtain a few more needed dollars from a penny-pinching City Council and state legislature, both of whom looked upon the Parkway experiment with a continually jaundiced eye.

So Bremer suddenly and quietly resigned on June 25, 1970, rather than go through the messy publicity of a public firing, or suffer a physical and mental breakdown from a continuance of his "suicide schedule."

Such an alternative would have hurt all the key personnel involved—and most importantly—the future stability of the Parkway Program.

After leaving Philadelphia, Bremer and his wife took a cabin in Pugwash, Nova Scotia, where he quietly worked for six months at writing his experiences at the Parkway. In February, 1971, Bremer was appointed Dean of the College of the Sacred Heart, a small Catholic girls' school, in nearby Newton, Massachusetts, where he is presently holding forth. This quiet campus presented a sharp contrast to the lively Parkway educational circus in Philadelphia where he had been in the center ring for two years.

One professional observer close to the program from the very beginning commented at Bremer's demise: "John tried to grab

[2] Ibid.

complete control of the Parkway in an arrogant way and he wound up without it. He and his staff got a big head after the first year and they paid the price for this folly."

Other critics noted that Bremer and the leadership of the Parkway Program took the stand that their evolving concept was "the cure and the solution to all educational problems." Their attitude caused serious grievances on the part of surrounding public school administrators and teachers who resented the fact that what innovations they were trying to inculcate into their schools were no longer considered relevant or important.

Cliff Brenner pinpointed Bremer's chief failure during his stormy two-year administration of the program wherein he made himself politically and professionally vulnerable to both Superintendent Shedd and the city council president. "Furthermore," observed the former administrative assistant to the president of the School Board, "as long as the Parkway Program dealt with a small percentage of students and did not attempt to disseminate what was worthwhile throughout the urban school system, its value remained a fringe benefit. If the educational goodies are not spread around the system, it has relatively little value."

"There was no excuse for Bremer cutting himself off from the school district and assuming an arrogant posture that he alone made the Program and that Shedd and [Dr. Bernard] Watson, the new Deputy Superintendent for Planning, had no brains to further his innovative concepts," said Brenner. "Bremer's position—that he was the only one with the correct wisdom to run the program— further alienated other key officials in the system, like Tom Rosica, the chief School Board liaison with the federal government."

Another school administrator close to the scene summed up Bremer's downfall with this tart phrase: "He brought it all on himself!"

One Parkway graduate summed up his feelings about the departed Bremer in a more positive way: "I *knew* John Bremer. He was a friend of ours. I couldn't really tell you what my old principal was like. He was a phantom. I have no regrets about my stay there, except that it wasn't longer."

In his own estimate of the situation, Dr. Shedd's major difference with Bremer over the running of the Parkway Program was a "fundamental and philosophical one." The superintendent's major educational goal was "to reshape the system, not to create a new one," which Bremer was trying to do. "I want to create alternatives in the system, hoping that these alternatives will force change," Shedd said emphatically in a personal interview.

Shedd, who was more of a traditionalist than Bremer, felt that the whole Parkway idea would have worked out better in practice if "it had been structured better." At the end of the first year, he felt that more "formality" was needed in carrying out the aims of the curriculum.

During postmortems, after Bremer's departure, Shedd was testy about his behind-the-scenes personality clashes with Bremer over differences of opinion expressed in public by the two educators over the direction of the Parkway Program. "It was *all* Bremer's fault," said Shedd angrily, "Not mine!" [3] (Bremer had, in turn, put most of the blame on Shedd for their inability to cooperate more peacefully and rationally on the growth problems of the Parkway Program.)

The bloody internal struggle between the two most powerful educational leaders in the Philadelphia school system almost brought about a premature death to the Parkway Program just as it was beginning to reach full flower. Fortunately only the heart of the flower was cut out, but the roots, stem, and petals remained.

[3] Author's interview with Dr. Shedd, July, 1969.

9. The Shift in Top Leadership

"The most deadly of all possible sins is the mutilation of a child's spirit."   *Erik Erikson* [1]

In retrospect, a fair assessment can be made that without the presence of the flamboyant Bremer, the Parkway Program may never have survived the first year. Once it was established and on firm foundations, there was a need for a settling down to bring some semblance of quiet order to the largely unstructured educational effort.

To keep the Parkway ship on an even keel, new leadership was needed and Shedd was prepared to fill the gap even before Bremer left the program. Dr. Leonard Finkelstein, the Principal of Sulzberger Junior High School and a former science coordinator in the Philadelphia school system, was quietly designated by the superintendent and the Board in the late spring of 1970 to be Bremer's successor. He was first appointed acting director of the Parkway complex for the 1970 summer program, and when Bremer resigned under pressure in late June, Finkelstein was moved up to full director of the Program.

Finkelstein, a low-pressure type in his early forties, had spent twenty years climbing the administrative ladder in the Philadelphia school system, starting out as a science teacher, then progressing to the post of a vice-principal, then principal, of a local elementary school before becoming a full principal at the junior high level.

Before taking over the reins, he anticipated that his primary problem at the Parkway would be one of establishing good rela-

[1] As quoted in Charles E. Silberman, *Crisis in the Classroom* (New York: Random House, Inc., 1970), p. 10.

tions with his fellow principals which had been almost "non-existent" under Bremer. "This situation hurt the internal public relations effort of the Parkway Program," he said candidly, "although those visitors from outside Philadelphia rarely learned this fact. When these other principals were asked questions about the Parkway at professional meetings or at other gatherings, they would have to answer with an embarrassed, 'I just don't know.' "

The new director vowed that he would try to overcome the jealousies and backlash that had plagued the internal professional relations of the school system vis-à-vis the Parkway. When asked why no school principals had spoken out about this situation heretofore, Finkelstein replied: "Most of them feared that if they criticized Bremer, it would appear in the local press and leave the false impression that they were against the Program—which was not true."

He also saw his task as one of helping to smooth out the interrelations within the school system, without jeopardizing the racial and economic mix of his student body.

To the outside world, the Parkway Program is still viewed as "Dr. Bremer's baby," according to the new director of the Program, but within the system, it is looked upon as "Shedd's baby." "The internal criticisms of the concept were 'triggered' mainly by anti-Bremer people scattered throughout the system," Finkelstein observed, "but they have died down since he left." (His prediction has held firm, since there has no longer been any hubbub over the Parkway Program emanating from within the system during the first ten months period of the new regime.)

Ironically enough, according to Finkelstein, who was a well-liked member of the Philadelphia school principals' establishment before assuming his new "hot seat" on the Parkway, most of his fellow administrators who were outspoken enemies of Bremer as a person were quiet supporters underneath of the school-without-walls concept. They knew that their public school system was in deep trouble and needed some sort of fresh academic adrenalin—which the Parkway provided.

"John may have created a mystique of tormentors within the system," said Finkelstein on the eve of his taking over the permanent Parkway directorship after Labor Day, 1970, "but now these enemies are supporters of what I will be carrying out. I feel that we can blend the best of the Parkway into the system soon to the mutual advantage of both, without prostituting the concepts of the program that I am about to direct."

One additional asset that Finkelstein had going for him was his close friendship with Cliff Brenner. While Bremer froze Brenner, the father of the Program, out of the picture once he took over the reins of the Program, Finkelstein brought him back in as a "kitchen cabinet" adviser.

On Sunday afternoons, as far back as 1968, Brenner and Finkelstein, who were both football buffs, sat together and plotted ways of making the unborn Parkway Program work effectively long before Bremer was hired for the task. These conversations paid off for Finkelstein when he finally found himself in the driver's seat in the most publicized high school in America in the early seventies.

Since the Parkway runs on a trimester plan, unlike the regular Philadelphia dual-semester plan, a regular summer session has been held each year since its founding. These sessions were not just make-up classes, which had been the predominant pattern in public school efforts held during the summer months, but rather an attempt to keep the regular curriculum alive during the hot months. Administration of the summer program was Finkelstein's first chore when he took over the Program.

A special summer program for all three units of the Parkway system was held in 1970 at the Alpha branch on Market Street. This limited effort, following the 1969 summer pattern, was aimed at keeping the Program operating in low gear during the intermission between the regular spring and fall school terms.

On July 6, 1970, over 100 students enrolled in Parkway classes due to the diligent efforts of a group of parents who obtained $5,500 from voluntary personal donations and from other interested groups to keep the Parkway going during the summer. (Pledges were made by over 250 concerned parents during a three-week phone solicitation period which took place in late June to insure that the program could open on schedule.)

Mrs. Kneeland McNulty, the Parkway's private fund-raising chairman, was amazed at the parental response to her request. "What was really impressive," she said, "was that every parent either pledged a cash contribution, or if they weren't in a position to help financially, they offered to donate their services."

Courses offered in the summer school catalog included such

100

new adventurous choices as "Alternatives in Journalism," "Sex Roles in American Society," "Man and the State," as well as a potpourri of courses offered in the regular curriculum.

The core of the summer program, however, was the establishment of two resource centers, one in math and the other in reading skills, both aimed at upping the quality of these basic learning tools for those students who felt they needed it.

In early 1970 Shedd expressed a "desire to establish an alternative to the present Parkway Program," by having mainly Junior Year (eleventh grade) students attend the Program and then return to their own schools for their senior year. "I do not see this alternative proposal as a *substitute*," he said candidly, "but as an *addition* to the present program. Meanwhile the three units will continue with their current effort—minus the elementary branch."

Finkelstein believed in going along with Shedd's idea to try an eleventh grade experiment on the Parkway in 1971, if possible. He felt that the one-year program deserved a try, but that it should not be looked upon as the only answer to the problem of selection and scheduling of students. "I mean to look for at least a dozen answers to our educational problems while I'm here," he said. "There is no one answer."

The Junior Year Parkway plan originally came from Monsignor Edward Hughes, (the local diocesan superintendent of schools) and not from the public school crowd. Dr. Finkelstein pointed out, "It could very well be the ninth year instead of the eleventh grade that turns out best in an experimental, one-year-only program. They are both worth trying."

In the fall of 1970, however, one official of the Parkway Program confirmed that "the Junior Year alternative approach is *not* getting anywhere here as far as we are concerned, since it was not *our* idea." This negative attitude on the part of the teaching staff would seem to doom Shedd's eleventh grade idea from becoming operational for the time being, although Dr. Finkelstein said at the time that he was willing to try it when the time was right.

There were other compelling reasons why the majority of the staff of the Parkway Program did not agree with Dr. Shedd's "single year at the Parkway" plan whether it encompassed the eleventh grade or some other high school grade level. Based on

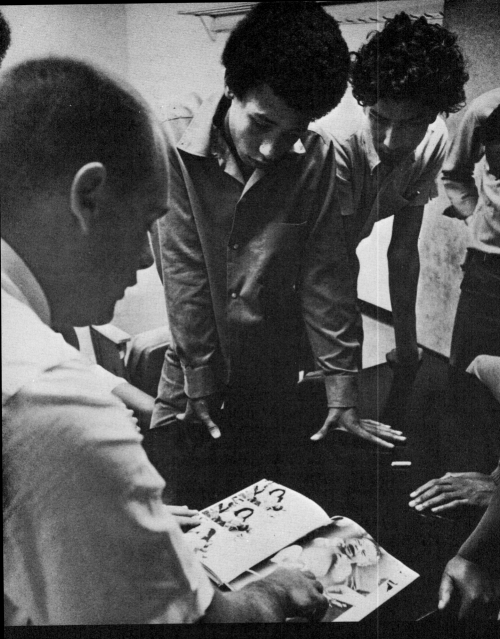
Students and teacher discuss child development.

their first two years' experience in the Program, they felt that not enough of the Parkway philosophy would rub off on the student in just one year's exposure before he was inserted back into the regular public or parochial school system.

One observer felt that it was presumptuous of some members of the Parkway staff to think that their "baby is the be all and end all" of educational innovations. Cliff Brenner, on the other hand, feels that *all* models should be tried to preserve flexibility in the effort.

Finkelstein was not content to stand still and just consolidate the gains made by his predecessor. He had some ideas of his own and hoped to build on the solid foundations erected by Bremer as soon as he could persuade the School Board and the community that the time was ripe for additional changes.

"I want to get the kids out of the Alpha, Beta, and Gamma branch centers and into Center City as soon as it is feasible," said Finkelstein confidently. "We can bus them to the cooperating facilities no matter where they are located."

The new director also believed that the use of the Antioch and other college interns at the Parkway has contributed a "tremendously important role to the success of the Program. [These interns] have provided an additional dimension to the course offerings by increasing the communications bridge between the students and faculty. This year the University of Massachusetts, Temple, and Cheyney State have joined the intern program." (Cheyney has a predominantly black student body.)

Dr. Finkelstein agreed with Bremer on the importance of the teacher and intern as a counselor in the tutorial effort to help the student with individualized human instruction instead of the impersonal machine teaching approach. "The Parkway teacher can learn with the students and not teach at them," he said. "We can make education a real two-way street and a new way of living in a school through this process." He sees the continuation of this relationship pioneered by Bremer as being very exciting and productive.

By mid-1970, some people agreed with the City Council president that the Parkway Program was a "crazy experiment" which should be abandoned forthwith. On the opposite extreme were those devout believers who saw the Parkway as an answer to all the problems of education.

103

In the middle was a group of citizens who were suspicious of this new thing in town—the "Everywhere School"—as some called it, where there was complete student freedom. This group thought the Parkway was somewhat weird, unworkable, and a waste of money.

In order to explode the myths that soon grew up around this pioneer educational experiment, Dr. Finkelstein worked quietly behind the scenes on a one-to-one basis to reestablish a better understanding with these diverse community groups as to what the Parkway was all about, rather than through the publicity media as his predecessor had done.

"City Council President D'Ortona is on very weak ground when he calls the Parkway Program a 'frill,' " said the new director. "Why should he say this when the Parkway is the most frugal, conservatively run school in the system? We have no plant, no upkeep, and no overhead. What we are doing will have an eventual feedback and economic savings for all the schools in the city."

Meanwhile, the much maligned and praised school without walls received a financial windfall. On February 8, 1971, the Board of Education accepted a $290,000 grant from the Ford Foundation for the expansion of the Parkway Program. According to Dr. Finkelstein, the funds would be used to implement expansion of the four-year program as it now exists with the use of additional facilities, teachers, and students; a one-year experience; geographic expansion; and a combination of these.

The expansion program began immediately with working models in the fall of 1971. The models were researched and developed by staff members who work in the various expansion programs. Personnel in the programs included Parkway teachers, teachers in Philadelphia's public schools, and applicants from other school districts.

Teachers received in-service training prior to the implementation of the various models. The training included teaching techniques used in the Parkway Program.

Expansion of the four-year program included the enrollment of 180 additional students, a larger teaching staff, and the rental of additional facilities in the Parkway area. All additional students were selected by lottery, as previous Parkway students had been.

In the geographic expansion model, a Delta branch of the

104

Parkway Program was opened in Germantown. Facilities were rented in that area and students attend classes as they do in buildings along the Parkway. The geographic area selected contains the necessary businesses and facilities for the various courses offered in the Parkway Program.

The one-year experience model, which was not established in 1971, would allow students to attend a Parkway-type school for one year. It would be designed for the student who needs educational motivation. Following the one-year experience, the student would return to his regular school.

The combination model might be a regular high school with a Parkway-type program attended by students from all parts of the city. It could include a built-in one-year program for certain students.

"We're not locked in to any particular type of expansion," said Dr. Finkelstein after receiving the grant, "but we may experiment with several different types. We may consider vertical expansion as well, such as a Parkway Middle-School program."

Although the Philadelphia School Board had been planning, with Finkelstein's and Kelner's approval, to open up a fourth, Delta, branch of the Parkway in the Northwest (Germantown) section of the city sometime in 1971, a surprise alternative agreement with the Southwest community groups in the Eastwick section was announced in March, 1971, to place the new branch in that part of town. This was a strange switch since Eastwick was also the home bailiwick of the City Council president, the most outspoken civic foe of the Parkway Program. The decision was also difficult to fathom in the light of the sparseness of industries, cultural institutions, and business enterprises in that formerly depressed section.

This new Eastwick Parkway plan was pushed by David Horowitz, the deputy superintendent of schools, who was known as the "hatchet man" for the School Board and the superintendent, when it came to firing people or burying innovative educational ideas. This alternative approach clearly did not represent the thinking of the Parkway staff or the Germantown groups who had been working the longest and hardest to expand the concept of their community first, and it did not come to fruition in 1971.

Meanwhile, plans were completed between Finkelstein, Kelner, and a group of Germantown parents to open the new branch of

105

the Parkway in the Northwest district in September, 1971. One hundred-fifty students could be accommodated in the new District Six unit (two-thirds, or one hundred, to be selected from public school applicants coming from within the district and the other fifty from public and private school students from outside the district).

To help publicize the selection process and the merits of the Parkway Program, teams of Parkway students and teachers made periodic visits to all senior, junior high, and upper elementary schools in the district to talk with prospective students.

On the broader question of expanding the Parkway Program as part of a metro-school system, Finkelstein saw the successful suburban school cooperation already established by his predecessor continuing. However, he realized that there was a problem of mutual exchange whenever the question of a predominantly white suburban school system's acceptance of black students from the city came up for consideration. He was hopeful that a management team could be sent to the suburbs to study the problems of regionalization and thus prepare the way for a greater expansion of the exchange of Parkway students with those of neighboring school systems in the near future.

Finkelstein also dreams of quietly reviving the controversial Paxson/Parkway elementary-secondary school. Although the old Paxson school was scheduled to be demolished in July, 1971, the Parkway director hoped that the authorities would postpone their decision one more year so that he could reinstitute the controversial program there.

Some critics have called the new Finkelstein era at the Parkway a compromise and a retreat back to the older, bureaucratically structured operation that was prevalent in the rest of the Philadelphia public school system. Actually, the so-called regression to the old academic order was only partial, since Finkelstein kept most of Bremer's innovations intact. His main new contribution was the reestablishment of necessary community relations contacts with his former colleagues, the estranged public school principals, who had been psychologically turned-off toward the experiment in their previous relations with Bremer.

The new leadership at the Parkway had made a smooth transition from the old buccaneer leadership of John Bremer—and the whole program received the positive fallout benefits.

Group of students on a field trip to a local business concern.

10. Crisis

"They [large high schools] are magnificent pyramids that will one day be wondered at."

Dr. John Bremer, December 9, 1969

In 1971 the Philadelphia school system suffered a series of blows which almost threatened its very existence. In the late spring, funds ran so low that the teachers received their last month's salary in scrip, which reluctant banks accepted as security for interest-free loans until a new fiscal year brought sufficient money to the district to redeem the scrip. With a $60 million deficit already on the books, the School Board faced the new school year with an estimated excess of expenses over income of $90 million.

The financial crisis was brought about by a combination of circumstances including spiraling costs of labor and teacher contracts, a sagging local tax base resulting from the continued flight of more affluent whites and industry to the suburbs, and highly uncertain assistance from other levels of government.

Local banks would no longer make any loans to meet unpaid bills. With its credit rating frozen, the School Board had to take drastic action to save the heart of the system. In June the Board announced that beginning in September, 1971, all interscholastic and intramural varsity sports were to be eliminated—including football, basketball, baseball, and track—drama and debating clubs were cancelled; and after-school art and music activities were also sacrificed. Kindergartens and the Parkway Program were saved, although many parents complained that these should have been eliminated to save the sports program. Also, the Board announced that 1200 school district jobs, including some 600 teaching positions, would be eliminated in this desperate attempt to bring the budget into line.

The proposed new Northwest unit of the Parkway Program almost suffered the same fate. The only thing that saved it was a promised $90,000 Ford grant that had been obtained by Northwest Philadelphia civic leaders to provide a needed extension of the Parkway Program in that area of the city. This broadening of the Parkway concept had been set for September, 1971, but Eversley Vaughn, the black president of the East Mount Airy Neighbors (EMAN) and the man who probably deserves the most credit for the extension, was told in late July, 1971, that the new program would be scrapped because of the budget cuts.

Three days later, the EMAN's executive secretary was informed that this decision had been reversed in the inner sanctums of the School Board and that the necessary money to operate the new center had somehow been "squeezed out" for the Program. Meanwhile School Board spokesmen were a bit more cautious when queried about the fate of the new Parkway effort, and they used words like "consider" and "investigate" to replace their previous official word "scrapped" when referring to the Program.

Bob Hutchins, the assistant director at the Parkway, said that the Board had seriously considered scrapping the Parkway extension because it "might not have been good politics to scrap one popular department, like sports, and expand something else," like the school without walls, which was less popular. [1]

William Jones, the director of public information for the School Board, replied that the nine-member board made a "complete turn-around" on this issue when they were denied much needed school funds by the city and state. They decided to investigate the Northwest program. This investigation could be interpreted as a subtle attempt to kill the idea by placing it on the shelf.

Although Jones felt that the Ford grant would be able to keep the new extension going, others at the Parkway Program itself, like Hutchins, claimed that this grant covered only necessary planning and expansion of facilities and did not cover the key operating expenses including teachers' salaries. Since the Board

[1] Bruce Ticker, "Crying Over the Schools' Cut of $1 Million," *Thursday's Drummer,* July 29, 1971, p. 5.

was committed to pay approximately $800 for the education of each public school child in the city, the new effort's budget would come to approximately $160,000—which was considerably more than the $90,000 Ford grant. [2]

Retiring Board President Dilworth had no comment on the controversial matter other than to hint quietly that the Program would open as scheduled in the fall of 1971.

The financial problems of the school system were compounded when the Pennsylvania state supreme court declared that the recently passed state income tax was unconstitutional. Much of the tax was to have gone for the besieged Philadelphia and Pittsburgh school systems. In addition to this loss of expected tax revenue, in July, Philadelphia's Mayor Tate vetoed a $13.8 million local liquor tax law that was aimed at helping the dying school system through the 1971-72 year. Even with the budget cuts, the School Board would be at least $68 million short for the coming year.

Not only were anticipated tax revenues lost to the schools, but the prospect of increased expenses also loomed on the horizon. The United States Supreme Court decision in the Pennsylvania parochial school case eliminated $9 million in state aid to the Philadelphia diocesan school district. Local Roman Catholic authorities had just announced a major hike in tuition for the coming year on the eve of the Court decision. Consequently, many Roman Catholic parents, who were already suffering from the inflationary spiral in the cost of living, thought twice before sending their children back to parochial schools in the fall. The enrollment in the Roman Catholic schools was significantly lower when they opened in September. The switch to public schools threw an added burden on the overstrained system.

Meanwhile, the Pennsylvania State Human Relations Commission issued a long-delayed order to integrate the entire Philadelphia de-facto segregated school system by 1974 at the latest. This decree would mean the bussing of some 50,000 school children a day in a system that was 60 percent black and 40 percent white. Board President Dilworth estimated that the cost of this program would be at least $40 million a year.

All of these financial difficulties were aggravated by the political infighting of the 1971 Philadelphia mayoralty election. Mayor

[2] *Ibid.*

Tate and his political heir apparent, ex-Police Commissioner Frank Rizzo, both issued edicts for Dilworth to resign and for Shedd to be fired. Tate even picked a heavily weighted anti-Shedd nominating panel to select new School Board members for 1972.

On the last day of June, the seventy-two-year-old Dilworth could take it no longer and announced that he would step down from the Board chairman's post in September and that he would resign from the Board two months early, in November, so that he could go out and work for the defeat of his fellow Democrat Rizzo. He was "frankly disturbed about the possibility" of Rizzo's becoming mayor and felt that the "candidate's statements are deeply disturbing to anyone who's interested in a good public education system."

Dilworth's resignation, when viewed in conjunction with the resignation of another Board member, who had spent over fourteen years on the School Board, meant that the outgoing mayor would have the power to select three new replacements who would undoubtedly be anti-Shedd and anti-Parkway since Tate had gone on record against such "frills" and innovations which he felt were irrelevant to a sound, well-disciplined educational system.

As the opening of school approached, there was a great deal of hue and cry about the sports program which had been cut from the fall schedule. In the context of the mayoralty race, the acting Board President, the Reverend Henry Nichols, wangled a promise from Mayor Tate, the Republican mayoralty candidate, Thacher Longstreth, and most of the candidates for City Council that they would all work for new city and state taxes to make up the budget deficit for the coming school year. The Democratic candidate, Frank Rizzo, wanted an opportunity to look for excess fat in the school budget before promising to seek new taxes. However, he did prod the owner of the Philadelphia Eagles professional football team, millionaire Leonard Tose, to offer $79,000 in cash toward the varsity football program in the schools. In return for these promises and the cash, Nichols encouraged the School Board to reinstate varsity sports and the entire extracurricular program. However, there was no guarantee that the promises would be fulfilled after the election and that the new tax money would be forthcoming so that schools could remain open for a full school year. Dr. Shedd commented on this reinstatement of the extracurricular activities by noting rather cynically: "I object

111

to people who get hysterical just because the great American pastime isn't going to happen here, but don't say a single word about the 600 teaching positions wiped out. It's a question of priorities." [3]

Furthermore, political and community pressures began to build for a revision of the Educational Home Rule Charter to eliminate the mayoral-appointed School Board and substitute an elected Board in its place. This drive was spearheaded by the outgoing mayor who had been unhappy with the actions of his appointed Board during the past four years.

In September, 1971, Dr. Shedd went before a congressional committee to plead for federal funding of the public schools as the only feasible way to overcome all of these financial-political problems. But somehow, through it all, Dr. Finkelstein and his cohorts kept the Parkway Program going in a low-key vein, while they continued to solidify and strengthen the Program for future onslaughts by its critics.

In keeping with its new, soft sell public relations approach engendered during the 1970-71 school year, the Parkway Program continued to provide a quiet contrast to the new school buildings that were being completed under the Dilworth-Shedd capital program. These latter multimillion dollar structures, such as the new Martin Luther King, Jr., High School, the Pickett Middle School, and the John B. Kelly Elementary School—to name a few—all seemed to give the appearance of windowless, cinder-block and brick fortresses that had turned their backs to the community.

These cold-looking, insulated edifices were purposefully designed without windows to help save high maintenance costs caused by replacing broken school windows and a rising vandalism rate that was dunning the public for several hundred thousand dollars annually. The students and vandals took quick advantage of these large monotonous walls, by freely and voluntarily decorating them in the dead of night or even defiantly in broad daylight with their own graffiti etched on the dull gray exteriors with multicolored spray can paint.

The Parkway Program presented just the opposite face to the community. It presented a large, open, "solid-glass" approach to

[3] Andrew H. Malcolm, "Football Escapes Philadelphia School Ax," *The New York Times,* September 21, 1971, pp. 1, 28.

the surrounding city to let the sunshine and learning in. In one sense, this stark contrast in physical plant symbolized the major differences in the philosophical approach to the curriculum between the system within the system and the dying traditional public school system.

Richard Saul Wurman, a thirty-six-year-old iconoclastic Philadelphia architect, designer, and civil leader, shares this view. The rotund, diminutive Wurman was not concerned with the possibility of the local public school closing down for lack of money.

"They're hopeless," he said with a sigh, "it's too late to correct them. Kids hate school. The truancy rate is 35 percent, despite what the city reports. It's an educational Vietnam.

"I want to spend a year studying alternatives. Why shouldn't the whole city be used in learning? Get the kids out of those walls. Parkway School is only one small experiment. Why not get 5,000 kids involved, out of that hostile environment?" [4]

Wurman is only one of a rising group of young civic leaders, who are not educators, who see in the Parkway concept a key to the future of deschooling society by breaking out of the bonds of the restrictive walls that now keep our children from learning about what the real world is like. In this respect, he, and others like him, will help to provide the necessary guideposts for the rebuilding of our educational system from the ashes of the current outmoded system that is no longer proving itself to be functional or practical for the complex times in which we live.

As one critic put it, schools, and not acid, speed, or junk, are the most destructive drug menace in our society today. Jerry Farber observed in his recent paperback book, *The Student as Nigger:*

> School is where you let the dying society put its trip on you. Our schools may seem useful: to make children into doctors, sociologists, engineers—to discover things. But they're poisonous as well. They exploit and enslave students; they petrify society; they make democracy unlikely. And it's not WHAT you're taught that does the harm but HOW you're taught. Our schools teach you by pushing you around, by stealing your will and your sense of power, by making timid, apathetic slaves of you—authority addicts.[5]

[4] From Sandy Grady, "Planner's Plea: Use Whole City for Learning," The *Sunday Bulletin* (Philadelphia), July 4, 1971.

[5] Jerry Farber, *The Student as Nigger* (Los Angeles: Contact Publishers, 1969).

This shocking analysis of our present dying public school system probably explains better than any other statement why nothing seems to be able to prevent the present crumbling from continuing in the immediate future. The hope is that new institutions —like the Parkway—can rise from the ashes to give tomorrow's generations a better opportunity than we had to grow up into mature adults in a peaceful world.

CHANGES IN ADMINISTRATION

Frank L. Rizzo was elected Mayor of Philadelphia in the 1971 election. The outgoing mayor appointed three persons to the School Board to fill vacancies so that the majority of the Board would be in sympathy with the policies espoused by Mayor-elect Rizzo. William Ross, a seventy-three-year-old labor union leader, was named President of the Board. The Board proceeded to negotiate a termination of its contract with Mark Shedd, and Matthew Costanzo was named to replace Shedd as Superintendent. Despite the change in top leadership, there was no immediate threat to the Parkway Program as a now-established part of the Philadelphia school system, since both Ross and Costanzo endorsed Shedd's innovative programs.

Parkway student observes a pasteurization process at a local bottling plant.

PART II
THE MEANING OF
THE PARKWAY
PROGRAM—ITS
IMPLICATIONS FOR
THE FUTURE OF
AMERICAN
EDUCATION

11. A Preliminary Evaluation of Education at the Parkway

"Without equal educational opportunity, we are not going to be able to solve society's handicaps. . . . To break the cycle of poverty, we have to harness the power of the schools. . . . There are hopeful signs of creative response in Philadelphia's Parkway high school." U.S. Senator Birch Bayh [1]

From the very beginning, the backers of the Parkway Program knew that evaluation of the Program would be the kingpin upon which its ultimate success or failure would rest. Silberman has pointed out that while it is still too early to make firm judgments about the Parkway Program's effectiveness, "the visitor cannot help but be impressed by the excitement Parkway has generated among its students." [2] Others who visited the complex came away with similar positive feelings.

Dr. Shedd believes it is healthy that the Parkway has remained *within* the system. "It's the most dramatic departure we've had in content and structure," he said in late 1970, "but it's too early to evaluate its results."

However, in its first two and one-half years of operations, the Parkway Program has made some remarkable contributions to its own evolving evaluation process, from which one can draw a fairly clear picture of the quality of total involvement of the students in the life of the city. An adequate evaluation of student progress has always been one of the strengths and weaknesses in the Parkway experiment.

[1] *The Evening Bulletin* (Philadelphia), April 5, 1971, p. 3.
[2] Charles E. Silberman, *Crisis in the Classroom* (New York: Random House, Inc., 1970), p. 355.

119

Even before the Program officially got underway in early 1969, Bremer said that he had no idea what the past performances of his first incoming student body had been and he didn't care to find out. "My job," he said during a television interview on the eve of the opening of the Alpha branch, "is not to evaluate their learning but to help them learn. Most schools reverse this process, and in general tend to de-motivate their students."

This rather narrow concept of Parkway student evaluation hurt the initial image of the Program in the eye of the old-line school administrators and tradition-minded teachers and parents. Bremer countered this pre-criticism of his plan with a retort that most present-day schools produce "triviality," which he promised would not be the case at the Parkway.

An intern from Antioch College, who spent a year on the Parkway, felt that the Program had been relatively "successful," but it had been "rough going" during the first year. "We need to wait and see if the school can survive politically in an urban setting, which is an external situation over which we have little control. Internally, however, we have been more successful in helping students to make important personal and academic choices."

The first informal evaluation of the Parkway Program occurred on the evening of June 3, 1969, when the Program was just three months old. Parents, teachers, pupils, and administrators met at the school administration building on the Parkway for a cold buffet supper to exchange ideas concerning the progress of the Program. There was much gaiety and lightheartedness as Bremer asked them to "compare notes with one another."

After admitting that several problems existed following the start of the Program, which had been mostly eradicated by late spring, both the parents and their children gave the Parkway Program a good rating at this meeting as the end of the first semester approached. Most parents praised the positive changes brought about in their children's attitudes as a result of the relaxed learning atmosphere at the various branches; a few complained about the lack of attention that routine subjects like biology and geometry were getting. Except for these minor criticisms, the Parkway Program passed its first general self-evaluation milestone with an excellent rating.

Evaluation at the Parkway is an ongoing process in which the

120

student must take at least as great a part as the teacher. Evaluation is one of the central courses of study at the Parkway. During their stay at the Parkway, the students must constantly evaluate their goals, needs, and objectives in order to choose new courses. It is a living part of the daily activity, not a postmortem which takes place after the damage has been done.

A formal evaluation takes place at the end of each semester, three times a year. During these sessions, students and faculty take time to discuss each student's progress and the Program's progress. Although no grades or marks are given, each student's record consists of narrative documents written jointly by the teacher and student in each course.

The written evaluation form usually consists of the teacher's description of the course evaluation of the work of the student, and also the student's evaluation of the course, the teacher, and his work in it. Reading lists, portfolios of significant work, and test scores, such as college boards, may be added. Three times a year, the whole packet is photocopied and issued as a "report card" by the student's tutorial leaders. The formal evaluation may take as long as two weeks. It is considered a part of the curriculum without which the other parts would be useless.

In place of the traditional grades, the Parkway staff evaluates its students with a "satisfactory completion" of work performed for purposes of college-bound transcripts. Failures are not recorded. Verbal evaluations of each student by his teachers are also an important part of the Program (and vice versa) to round out the process. Because of the great diversity of the student body, it is still too early for faculty members to make any long-range, valid predictions about which students stand the best chance of "making it" in the wider world.

There has been some criticism of the Parkway Program which bears watching as the enterprise matures. Silberman believes that there was "a certain intellectual flabbiness in a great many of the courses being offered during the first semester," but was assured by Bremer that this "flabbiness" was only temporary. [3]

He further noted after his visit to the Program in 1969, that there was a "tendency, observable in other programs, for teachers, once they are released from the rigidities of the traditional curriculum and school organization, to swing to the opposite extreme,

[3] Silberman, *op. cit.*, p. 354.

Student studying in the gaily decorated locker room at Alpha Branch.

turning classes into extended 'rap sessions.' " Silberman believes that most students and their teachers tire of this constant, unstructured, free discussion atmosphere fairly rapidly and ultimately seek to return to more structured curriculum approaches. [4]

There was some diverse opinion among the faculty and Bremer during the first year at the Parkway on the question of combining the functions of instruction and tutorial guidance sessions, believed in by the latter but not by the former.

Furthermore, Bremer's insistence that only "starting points" should be prescribed for students and not the "goals," which freely translated by the students meant that the Parkway was a place where "every student did his own thing," also added fuel to the "flabbiness" charge by the Parkway's critics.

After the shakedown period, one of the major differences between the Parkway and the regular high schools appeared in the "course selection" category. The Parkway gives the student a much wider latitude in picking his courses from the catalog in order to meet the minimum state requirements for graduation.

Some parents worried that the Program did not deal adequately enough with the basic skills while others had anxieties that their children were not independent enough to handle the increased freedom and responsibility; that they often floundered and needed more direction. A few students confessed that some classes soon degenerated into bull sessions, while others quickly turned into routine lectures. When the latter happened, the students were quick to call the teachers to task for it.

Only a few of the cooperating institutions have complained so far about the Parkway students being a nuisance. These are invariably industries and local businesses who complained about abuses of equipment or facilities. Only one cultural institution, the Ethical Society, on Rittenhouse Square, closed its doors to Parkway students after a series of robberies, which were attributed to them by Society officials.

Several of the courses offered by the local business and industrial establishments did not work out in practice; so they were quietly dropped from the flexible curriculum. Today there are relatively few courses at the Parkway not taught by Parkway teachers—wherever they hold forth—but the innovations in these courses still include the use of the cultural institutions.

[4] *Ibid.*

123

The average daily attendance at the Parkway is 89 percent, which is substantially higher than the 75 percent to 80 percent average of the other city high schools. This figure is even more noteworthy when it is realized that the school day at the Parkway is considerably longer—from 9 to 5 for some students—than it is for the regular schools which usually finish at 3:00 P.M. (Those high schools on double sessions end the school day even earlier—at 12:30 P.M.)

The dropout rate is practically nonexistent at the Parkway while it runs as high as 35 percent on the average in the regular city high schools. This statistic alone speaks well for the educational worth and value of the Program. Since any student can leave the Program at will—because *all* have volunteered for the experiment—this loyalty to the Parkway is the best testimony so far to its feasibility and relevancy.

The percentage of Parkway students who go on to college already appears to be higher than that of the regular Philadelphia secondary schools. Of 80 students who graduated in June, 1970, 42 applied for college and 20 were accepted before May 1. Of the first eight graduates who completed their work in February, 1970, two had jobs with an insurance company by May, and four were in college. Two others planned to enroll in college in the fall of 1970.

As of January, 1972, about 50 percent of the Parkway graduates have gone on to college, compared with about 35 to 40 percent from the whole school system. Most of them have done outstanding work in college, and the only criticism from their colleges is that they want to bring about change too rapidly.

Significantly, of those Parkway students who have gone on to college from the first two graduating classes, the dropout rate has been much smaller than that for regular high school graduates. This is a healthy sign that the Parkway Program is working since it represents a true cross section of the entire Philadelphia high school student body and not just an elite finishing school for the upper classes only. Though many students had behavioral problems in their previous school, discipline problems at the Parkway have proved minimal. With so much freedom, what about self-discipline? Again, Bremer saw no problem. The program "forces" self-discipline on the student by making him realize that if he is to get the job done in the way that he wants, he will need self-discipline. He realizes that he is part of a learning team and that he must cooperate with and not compete against anyone else.

While the educational pluses outnumber the minuses at the Parkway, there have been a few items of dissatisfaction expressed by the students. One felt that "some teachers have a problem of adapting to the new system, and a few just can't seem to make the transition from the old way of doing things."

"It is harder for the teachers than for us," commented another student sadly, "because they are usually so set in their ways."

"But we don't curse at them here," a pretty co-ed said, "even if they are not on our wavelength and don't make it, because, here at least, they try."

Other minor complaints rendered by the Parkway students, such as the subpar physical conditions of their "homeroom" buildings with the paint peeling off the walls, whether it is the prototype, Community Alpha, or the old Paxson elementary school, the lack of a full-time school nurse, and other similar gripes, are few in number. These drawbacks are overshadowed, however, by the positive contributions of the Program which keep the students' morale at a high level.

One sixteen-year-old black youth who was asked if he had learned more at the Parkway than in his former school answered: "Yes, I really think so, because I'm starting to pay attention here. Learning is more personal and interesting here instead of having to listen to a dictatorial teacher saying: 'You'll learn this or else! And after you put what I told you down on a test paper, I'll grade it and you'll either pass or fail!'

"Here the atmosphere is more relaxed and the material is spiced up so that you really want to dig it. I even fought my mother to come here on bad weather days when it was sleeting or snowing, because I knew I wasn't just going to hear a teacher go 'blah, blah, blah' from 9 to 3, but that I was going to learn something that would help me. Funny, I had the worst attendance record in my old school, being absent 110 days last year, but here, I haven't missed a day."

The first outside evaluation of the Parkway was conducted in May, 1970, by Professor Albert Oliver and his team from the University of Pennsylvania. Oliver, who serves in the Curriculum and Instruction Department of the Graduate School of Education at Penn, chaired a committee of five people who made the three-day evaluation of the Parkway Program, at Finkelstein's request. In a 15-page report which was given to the Board in July, they made some positive recommendations to the School Board concerning the school without walls.

Their first concern was their failure to discover any organized statement of the philosophy behind the program other than short statements made by Bremer to the press. "So we formulated our own purposes as we discerned them," said Oliver, "and came up with ten different student-oriented goals."

"The most important of these was the ability to develop skills in decision making. The typical school does not give the students an opportunity to make their own decisions, but we found that the Parkway was doing a good job in this area," concluded the Penn professor.

In the tutorial area, the Oliver committee found "tremendous variations" in the way the counseling tutorials were run in each of the three houses (Alpha, Beta, and Gamma). "Too often, these periods became rambling rap sessions," they discovered.

The evaluators also found that basic skills needed greater emphasis and that administrative reins needed tightening. "John Bremer was a laissez-faire man on this point," Oliver opined, hoping that Finkelstein would do something about it (which he has).

In concluding that the pluses outweighed the minuses in their overall evaluation of the Program, the committee discovered that students who had previously attended Girls' High and Central High showed better attendance and motivation at the Parkway, where they had "formerly been dragging along in their old schools."

Before he left, Bremer had also instituted a comprehensive, ongoing internal evaluation system beginning in early 1970. This unique approach not only made use of new creative devices instead of the old-fashioned tests, but assessments were made when students had to negotiate for material things like classroom space. Further research was started on how Parkway students differed in their relations to adults and teachers compared to those who attended regular schools.

To accomplish this goal, Bremer planned to have ten Parkway students randomly selected and compared with ten others who would be selected from traditional public schools in an adult situation. The purpose of the exercise was to identify *how* and *why* the typical Parkway students appeared to be more persuasive and better motivated.

As far as comparing the reading ability of his students with those of similar students in regular public and private schools by giving each of them a battery of Iowa tests, Finkelstein felt it would be an exercise in futility. "Forget it," he said curtly. "We are dealing with things at the Parkway far more important than percentile ratings."

One fascinating facet of evaluating the whole Parkway experiment which was overlooked by most of the visiting educators who flocked to the Program, was a point-by-point comparison with another, less well-publicized, innovative, educational experiment that was housed just across the street from the gray, somewhat dilapidated stone building housing the Parkway's Community Alpha. High up in the new gleaming white skyscraper known as the IVB building, named for the Industrial Valley Bank, the offices of the Research for Better Schools, Inc., can be found. This multimillion dollar, federally financed, regional educational research agency has focused its main task on the implementation of the concept of Individually Prescribed Instruction (IPI) throughout the public and private schools of America.

This Research for Better Schools organization, headed by Dr. James Becker, the former Associate Superintendent of Research for the School District of Philadelphia, is in direct competition with the Parkway Program as far as pioneering any innovations in learning and educational evaluation of students is concerned.

Where the Parkway aims at ultimately measuring what we say we are after, the RBS/IPI approach is to go after things that can be measured. Becker and his cohorts *"reject the idea that maximum freedom is a necessary condition for something called the individualization of instruction,"* [5] while the Parkway follows a reverse approach.

In stark contrast with the Parkway Program, the IPI approach allows no room for the achievement of individual learning behavioristic goals in art, music, drama, or any other subject, but only the rigidly specified and subjective ends of the IPI/RBS moguls. The major weakness of their approach is similar to that

[5] Silberman, *op. cit.*, p. 199, excerpted from James Becker, *Harvard Educational Review*, Fall, 1968. Italics in original.

of the educational behaviorists who have ordained that the goals of education should be defined in narrow behavioristic terms. Silberman points out that this teaching machine oriented educational theory is appropriate for training in industry or the military but not for educational purposes. Those who profess that what is needed is improvement of the so-called "state-of-the-art" of the IPI system are not being realistic, since the whole basic assumption of this program is false. IPI is training, not education, while the Parkway is the opposite.

IPI's strategy assumes that the educational ends are known as opposed to the Parkway's open-ended approach to learning. Programmed instruction, as propounded by the IPI, can teach rote learning, but not reasoning. It is a clever, gimmicky way of getting data force-fed into children's minds. But this methodology is only part of the whole educational process. The IPI approach rules out the important inter-learning relations between the pupil and the teacher, substituting a new pupil/machine relationship in its place. Under IPI, student achievement is defined as something limited to what the student can learn in one class period.

Silberman makes a devastating critique of Becker, Robert Glaser, their IPI oriented associates, and of the program as it is practiced in 164 schools in 33 states in the 1969-70 school year. In the *Crisis in the Classroom,* he claims that Becker's definition of educational alternatives represents a misunderstanding of its goals. He then proceeds to conclude that: *"What is undesirable about IPI is precisely that it does not permit any position between the two extremes* [freedom and lack of freedom in pursuing educational goals]; *the instructional technology can work only if those who write the programs specify every goal in the most precise and detailed terms."* [6]

Although the IPI has expanded more rapidly than the Parkway (with over 1000 cities on the waiting list in early 1971), it has not fared as well at the hands of the educational critics. The major fallacy of IPI, which has received almost as much nationwide publicity as the Parkway Program, can be found in the emphasis on the word "prescribed." What the individual student accomplishes must be prescribed in such narrow terms that no room is left for exercising his individuality.

The Parkway Program, on the other hand, provides a healthy

[6] Silberman, *op. cit.,* p. 199. Italics in original.

Two students in deep thought—locker room Alpha.

alternative antidote for the IPI system by allowing the student to strike out on his own. Where the IPI has its restricted limits, the Parkway is unlimited. "We haven't thought much about what kind of citizens the school is going to turn out," confessed Glaser, "while the Parkway cares about this goal." [7] Furthermore, the IPI "forces students into a passive, almost docile role, under the name of individualization," according to Silberman, [8] while the Parkway encourages the opposite, activist role for its students.

In one sense, it can be said that Market Street in Philadelphia, which separates the offices of the Parkway Program from those of the IPI, represents the widest street in the American educational world of the 1970s, just as 120th Street in Manhattan performed a similar philosophical function in the twenties and thirties, separating Teachers College of Columbia University, both physically and philosophically, from the main liberal arts branch of that institution of higher learning.

The late Reverend Russell Conwell founded Philadelphia's Temple University in 1884 with the benefit of hundreds of thousands of dollars brought in from his famous Chautauqua circuit lecture: "Acres of Diamonds." In that historic lecture, the nineteenth century Baptist preacher exhorted his audiences to look in their own backyards and they might strike oil or other riches there, instead of going off to some foreign land in search of wealth. Similarly, it appears strange that the sophisticated educational researchers of RBS and IPI are so wrapped up with the computerized prospects of their new technology that they have had no time to examine the far more fruitful educational prospects learning and walking about on the streets below while attending the school without walls. The irony of this situation, highlighted by the lack of cooperation and communication between these two innovative educational giants, presents one of the sad commentaries on the present, largely rudderless, state of American education.

One veteran education administrator, who served as a consultant in the planning phase of the Program, cautioned that the ultimate success or failure of the Parkway concept will depend largely on the evaluation system used to test students' academic competencies and learning skills.

How can independent study be properly evaluated? Can the

[7] *Ibid.,* p. 200.
[8] *Ibid.,* p. 201.

tutors offer effective remediation? Is there enough self-motivation in the average student so that he can extend himself on his own—as the Program assumes that he will?

Some observers have called the Parkway approach an overly simplistic, naïve, or "Utopian" solution to the urban educational bind. First of all, they argue that the Program doesn't begin to provide a solution to the more complex problems urban schools are confronting—such as teachers who are inadequately trained and students who are burdened by the physical and psychological effects of poverty. They question, too, the educational validity of the courses offered at the city's institutions and wonder whether institutional personnel are really equipped to be teachers, or just competent public relations men and tour guides.

These are some of the questions still to be answered in the young Parkway experiment. The final report card will not be in for several years. But the school's supporters are confident that when it does come out, it will, at the very least, credit the Philadelphia program with an innovative attempt to gear education to needs of youngsters who will be living the bulk of their lives in the twenty-first century.

12. Parkway Spin-Offs

"Our second wish is that every man should be wholly educated, rightly formed not only in one single matter or in a few or even in many, but in all things which perfect human nature."

John Amos Comenius,
The Great Didactic, 1632 [1]

Cliff Brenner believes that the Parkway idea has already gained wide acceptance in American educational circles for the practicality of its basic concept. "People in urban and some suburban areas can see applications in their own settings more clearly," he said, looking back on the first two years of its operation.

"The Parkway concept does *not* say that you must have a set of cultural institutions in close geographical proximity, only that you have *no* adequate school building in the neighborhood. There are countless environments that can and should be utilized to save space and money as well as to ease the rigidity of the present public educational system," he concluded.

Since the inauguration of the Parkway Program in February, 1969, there have been several direct, tangible spin-offs that have taken place in the Philadelphia school system as well as some interesting intangible offshoots that are also worth examining. Furthermore, the Parkway's magnetic attraction has already spread its tentacles to the college campus and to other cities like New York and Milwaukee, where similar schools without walls are either already operating or are in the planning stage. (Each of these Parkway spin-offs will be examined briefly in this chapter.)

[1] Quoted in Charles Silberman, *Crisis in the Classroom* (New York: Random House, Inc., 1970), p. 3.

TANGIBLE PARKWAY SPIN-OFFS

Project Learn (The resurrection of the Paxson/Parkway in Germantown)

After the Paxson elementary branch of the Parkway was closed in the dispute with the Board and Shedd, the parents moved their children to some unused Sunday school rooms of the Germantown Unitarian Church rather than return them to the public schools. They dubbed their new school Project Learn and operated it successfully for a year on a shoestring budget at that location before moving to another church up the street.

Fifty children attended the innovative elementary school in two stone buildings set in a grove of tall oaks and rhododendrons in a park-like setting behind the main church. It operated daily from 9 to 3 with the parents administering the school, transporting the children, and doing most of the teaching. The only paid staff were four full-time teaching faculty members including two certified teachers and two teaching aides. Students from Antioch College, the University of Pennsylvania, and Temple University also contributed their free time, serving as interns in a similar capacity to that of their fellows on the Parkway.

Those parents who could afford it paid $35 a month to help defray the overhead of the school, including a nominal rent to the church for the use of its utilities and facilities. Although the state education department failed to recognize the school as either a legitimate public or private institution during the first year of its operations, this roadblock did not deter the parents, staff, or children.

Although Dr. Shedd reluctantly agreed in the early spring of 1970 to seek a small $10,000 grant of foundation funds to help see them through the remainder of the year, he failed to come through on his promise.

The major aim of the school in the words of the director, Mrs. Caroline Snyder, was "to create a child who can find out who he is."

When Project Learn moved to the first floor and basement of Epiphany Episcopal Church in Germantown, critical observers were impressed at the cooperative effort of both the staff and the upper elementary children (fourth to sixth graders) in helping the

133

younger first to third graders get off to a better educational start than their public school peers.

A sophomore intern from Oberlin College and a junior intern from that same school were enthusiastic over the possibilities of Project Learn. They and six other college interns helped to make it possible to keep learning groups in the small church cubicles down to an ideal class size of eight to ten students. This number was much more favorable than the thirty plus students in comparable public schools in Philadelphia.

By its second year Project Learn had settled down on a semi-structured basis, where a new group of students began a fresh project every two weeks. After the teachers listed five areas of possible learning, the students would pick one for intensive study. For instance, a third grade group decided to make chocolate-chip cookies but instead of purchasing ready-made mix from the supermarket, they bought raw wheat and ground it into flour (with a meat grinder). They also went to a local chocolate factory where they were given some cocoa and vanilla beans, and they visited the local library where they found some cookbooks.

"When the children understand what they are doing and why, they learn more and are better motivated," said one of the teachers. "Important things are happening here in education, particularly the emphasis on small group learning."

Instead of being divided into the usual six elementary grade levels, Project Learn was broken up into three broader groupings: thirty children at the fifth and sixth year age level in the lower branch; thirty in the middle branch comprising the seven- to eight-year-olds and thirty in the upper branch who were nine- to twelve-year-olds.

The afternoon program at Project Learn was divided into special interest areas, i.e., reading, math, or writing. In the morning, the children chose what they would do in the afternoon. On certain days, specific courses in pottery, cooking, bread baking, arts, metal work, craft work, and basket weaving were offered to provide variety and spice to the curriculum. Gymnastics were held on two afternoons each week.

Most teachers are informally dressed at Project Learn, following in the footsteps of their predecessors on the Parkway. Most of the women wear blue jeans or slacks.

Project Learn has had its problems, however. With no formal

textbooks or guidelines, some of the students and teachers often get lost academically, but they do not retreat into apathy.

"All things are experimental here," said one of the interns. "And we are still not sure of what we are doing. This is different from Summerhill. The kids are not completely free here to do what they want to do all of the time—as they did over there."

"The kids who come to Project Learn are expected to treat others like human beings," the other Oberlin intern chimed in. "If they want to stay home, that's O.K. They are not looked upon as truants."

The parents and staff of Project Learn are concerned that their children are not in a legal school as far as the Commonwealth of Pennsylvania is concerned. They get around the state laws at present through a loophole that permits home tutoring; so no truant officer comes knocking to take their children back to the despised public schools.

Children in Project Learn study the principles of mathematics through learning how to apportion recipes so as to mix the proper amount of batter for cakes and cookies as well as computing problems and figures on a piece of paper.

"Hard-core math," said one of the certified teachers, "is adding up the grocery store bill."

She also explained that instead of all the children reading from the same textbook, Project Learn gives each child his or her own choice. "Children will read something they are interested in," she said.

Among other things discussed by the older children in Project Learn, besides the normal classroom routine, were gardening techniques and the meaning of the classic folk-rock Broadway musical "Hair," which several of the students had seen with their parents.

Project Learn students are also encouraged to write, stage, produce, and act in their own plays. One of them was called the "Invisible Brave"—a fantasy on race relations centered around the problems of black and white Indian squaws who each wanted to become the wife of the "Invisible Brave." The children worked facts on Indian lore, dress, and customs into their fascinating script.

Mrs. Snyder said that she and her cohorts found it difficult to

135

get the foundation money that Dr. Kelner had promised to try and obtain for them since "we are illegal and are neither public nor private."

"Dr. Shedd passes the buck to Kelner and the district superintendent refuses to give us any money," complained one frustrated parent/teacher. "We are going to try and force some meaningful funding from the Board of Education for 'Project Learn' as a 'legitimate public school alternative' before we take out a private school charter. It is tricky to make our real needs known to Shedd since he has become so insulated from the community by his own bureaucracy. Some of us feel that the school administration is trying to divide us by pitting Project GASP (Germantown Area School Project) against the proposed Northwest branch of the Parkway Program so that neither of us can win."

Dr. Kelner defended his actions vis-à-vis the progressive Germantown parents by stating that he met with Snyder and the other parents on twenty-seven occasions. "They would not give in to the necessary controls demanded by the school district of Philadelphia in return for the money, certification, and our blessing," he said. "They also would not agree to a random selection of students so that we could bring more blacks in. I bent over backwards to meet their demands, but they wouldn't compromise."

Meanwhile, Project Learn staggered on from day to day, hoping that one day soon it would win recognition to enhance its survival.

The West Philadelphia Community Free School

A year after the birth of the Parkway Program, a second similar innovative educational effort got off to an inauspicious start less than a mile away under the guise of the West Philadelphia Community Free School. This latest secondary experimental offshoot from the Philadelphia public school system owed a deep debt of gratitude to its cousin on the Parkway, whose prior success helped the Free School to come alive despite the handicaps of its oft delayed opening.

Cliff Brenner believes that the West Philadelphia Community Free School, which came to life on one lung in early 1970, would never have come into being without the foundational impetus laid by the Parkway Program.

136

The Free School was technically the brainchild of Dr. Aase Eriksen, an assistant professor of education at the Graduate School of Education at the University of Pennsylvania. She thought of the idea of translating the Friskoler (Free School) concept from her Danish homeland to West Philadelphia in the area bordering the University of Pennsylvania's burgeoning campus. The school was first scheduled to open on November 1, 1969, with four hundred overflow students drawn from West Philadelphia High School, but bureaucratic roadblocks prevented the formal opening until February, 1970.

The "Eriksen Plan" to establish a Free School in Philadelphia was not modeled directly after the Parkway Program, but rather from a conglomerate of ideas of which the Parkway was an important one. Basically it is derived from the nineteenth century Danish schools established by dissatisfied parents as an alternative to the state's regular schools. In time they grew in number and popularity, until today they carry a major share of Danish childhood education.

The West Philadelphia Community Free School also owed part of its origins to the demands of the predominant black majority in the community who for their own children wanted a program which was not white middle-class oriented. Mrs. Novella Williams, the chairman of the parents' group, reasoned that there was room for a second school without walls that could be located in her part of the city.

This institution, like the Parkway, was also under the jurisdiction of the Board of Education, although it was not the direct brainchild of the Board, but rather of the West Philadelphia community and the university. The Board of Education leased two old houses and the Free School parents helped to fix them up for classroom use in the area of Thirty-ninth and Walnut Streets adjacent to the Penn campus. The Board also leased a room in the Philadelphia Civic Center, which was used primarily for commercial exhibits, and ultimately hoped to expand the facilities so that up to one thousand students could be comfortably situated somewhere in the scattered Free School complex.

The plan was to have each house contain seven teachers and a head teacher to be drawn from the West Philadelphia High School. The teachers were chosen by the community representatives in consultation with the principal of West Philadelphia High,

137

Walter Scott, and District Superintendent Dr. Marechal-Neil Young, a black educator.

Like the Parkway Program, in the nongraded Free School the students proceeded to learn at their own pace. The curriculum pattern which came out of the community planning conferences with Dr. Eriksen was similar to the Parkway in that the school would teach basic skills in the houses for half the school day while allowing the students also to pursue career training in local industries. Some of the students also spent time at the university and allied businesses learning about the law, the market, and insurance.

When the school finally opened for business on February 2, 1970, the first two hundred students had to convene in one of the university auditoriums and then split up into "families" of fourteen to each teacher. They could not go into their newly rented houses because of a zoning problem bottleneck over the lack of adequate fire escapes; so they temporarily moved their operations to the West Philadelphia Branch of the Free Library, some unused rooms in the University City Science Center, and rooms in two area churches.

Some of the West Philadelphia Community Free School students learned about clinical laboratory services at the nearby Veterans Administration Hospital. Others soon went to the Philadelphia Divinity School, where they researched the causes and solutions to a growing drug problem in the area. By early 1971, over five hundred students, many of whom were dropouts from other area high schools, were attending the nongraded classes of the West Philadelphia Community Free School.

Significantly, at the opening brainstorming session of the new institution, the students soon found themselves engaged in an animated discussion of the Vietnam War—how we got into it; why we are there; and how we might get out. This discussion did not take place in a conventional classroom, but rather in the Free School's hallway on a cold rainy day.

Although the West Philadelphia Community Free School was not the first such institution of its kind to be established in the United States (dozens of others were already in existence across the country), its closeness to the Parkway Program and the University of Pennsylvania put it automatically on a pedestal where it would bear watching as it progressed.

138

". . . perhaps the greatest achievement of these [free] schools," wrote Bonnie Barrett Stretch, an associate education editor of *Saturday Review,* "is with the parents. They develop a new faith, not only in their children but in themselves. 'Now I know,' said a New York City mother, 'that, even though I didn't finish high school, it is possible for me to understand what they are teaching my child.' In changing their children's lives, these parents have discovered the power to change their own lives, as well." [2]

Many of these parents who are not working as aides or coordinators often drop by the informal classroom to see how their children are doing, something they would not have thought of doing in the regular schools.

This enthusiastic parent involvement was noticeably apparent at both the Parkway Program and the West Philadelphia Community Free School.

By February, 1971, a year after the West Philadelphia Community Free School officially got under way, some 480 students were happily enrolled in one of the three converted houses which the School Board had rented for their use. With its full-time teachers and a handful of black and white volunteers to assist them, the Free School ushered in Philadelphia's "junior" Parkway with a minimum of furor and a maximum of excitement and community support.

The School Board showed its faith in the program by underwriting it for $109,000, with an additional $60,000 donated by the University of Pennsylvania and $20,000 contributed by the West Philadelphia Community.

"Because of these new facilities," said Mrs. Novella Williams, the founder of Citizens for Progress, who spearheaded the Free School project in the community, "there no longer are any double-shifts at the West Philadelphia High School. We've also been able to develop successfully a different kind of school within the confines of the public school system."

The Durham Learning Center

A second attempt to establish a pseudo-elementary school without walls within the Philadelphia public school system was

[2] Bonnie Barrett Stretch, "The Rise of the 'Free School,'" *Saturday Review,* June 20, 1970, p. 92.

139

quietly instituted in the abandoned, formerly all-black Durham Elementary School in South Philadelphia in September, 1970.

The Durham Child Development Center is under the direction of Dr. Peter Buttenwieser, the former head of the highly successful North Carolina and Pennsylvania Advancement Schools. The Durham Center is a unique public school with an innovative educational program that was modeled after both the Parkway Program and the British Infant School System.

This new center is open all day Monday to Friday, plus three nights a week and Saturday mornings as well, to children (and adults) from all parts of the city and the nearby suburbs.

The Durham Child Development Center, which was created by a Board of Education resolution on July 27, 1970, made significant progress during its first year of full operations. Five interrelated programs took place daily from dawn to after dark in the four floors of the abandoned Durham elementary school located on the edge of a ghetto area in South Philadelphia. These programs included: the *Infant Center,* which catered to a dozen babies under eighteen months and a similar number of toddlers from eighteen months to three years of age; the *School-age Mothers' Center* for teenage mothers, where some 18 participated in the first year; the *Head Start Program* of prekindergarten education which served some 50 children; the *Learning Center Program* (K-4), which provided opportunities for 150 children coming from five other elementary schools located within a mile radius of the center; and finally the *Teacher Center,* where teachers and parents could make their own equipment and materials to teach their children.

The integration of these activities under one roof, particularly those of the joint parent-toddler learning in the modified daycare adult learning center, was faintly reminiscent of the defunct Paxson/Parkway elementary-senior high joint educational effort. The psychological impetus provided by the Parkway Program, not only of its successes, but also of its failures, aided such less publicized local innovative educational efforts as the Durham Center to progress and experiment at their own pace with similar and different offshoots from those tried at the Parkway.

Dr. Buttenwieser summed up a question that he and his staff had to keep asking themselves during the first year at Durham: "Does it all make sense? Can we establish five different programs in a way that strengthens each of them?" He answered these questions with an emphatic: "Yes!"

The continuing education of teenage mothers at Durham helps to prevent them from becoming permanent dropouts of the system while at the same time gives them a chance to be close to their young children next door in the nursery. While their babies are being cared for in the Infant Day-Care Center, the young mothers and mothers-to-be are learning a great deal of practical information about child care and child growth and development, as well as maintaining their own scholastic development.

(One of the projects worked on by a group of expectant teenage mothers at the Center included the making of ninety cradles for their own and other newborn disadvantaged babies. Since there were a minimum of 1000 such infants born to school-age children each year in the public schools of Philadelphia, this project met a felt need.)

Some infants enter Durham as early as one month, or as soon as their pediatrician recommends their release. Mothers visit and play with their newborn children several times during the day and are encouraged to feed them lunch. It is an ongoing educational experience for both the mothers and the babies in which the invisible walls between the home and school are merged into one.

The toddler program is a simulated home experience brought into the school. It includes group playtime, independent play, lunch (where the students often feed themselves), hall play, nap time, and story time.

At the teacher center, teachers, aides, parents, and children are free to come at any time of the day and night to use materials and equipment which they can build and create into finished products that they can take away to their homes or schools.

The concept of the five-segment Durham Child Development Center did not stem directly from the Parkway Program but rather from the experiences of Mrs. Lore Rasmussen in her small learning lab approach to early childhood education. This low-keyed effort progressed in just five years from a few hours a day in one pilot elementary mini-school to an all-day model program, then all week long, until the Durham Center was launched officially in the summer of 1970.

Utilizing an abandoned elementary school that "was up for

grabs," according to Dr. Peter Buttenwieser, since the School Board had originally wanted to convert it into administrative offices for the local district superintendent, the Durham Center has matured in one year to where it is already being looked upon as one of the foremost learning centers of its kind in America—despite its low visibility approach.

"We profited from the high-visibility experiences of the Parkway Program," said the Durham director, "and decided for 'political' reasons to present an opposite profile to the public until we got on our feet. We were influenced indirectly by the pioneering efforts of the Parkway Program, even though we had little direct contact with John Bremer. We profited from their mistakes—particularly at the Paxson/Parkway, since we were attempting to create a comprehensive child development center and knew there would be opposition out there from those who did not understand what we were trying to accomplish."

Utilizing techniques pioneered at the turn of the century at Tuskegee Institute by the late Dr. George Washington Carver, the students, parents, and teachers at the Durham Center made periodic raids of trash baskets and garbage cans to obtain material to use as the basis of their craft projects.

The educational atmosphere at the Durham Center has been described as "commune-like," in that families are being educated together under the same roof. The student body at Durham is 65 percent black and 50 percent from poor, low-income families. They are bussed in by public transportation from their homes in scattered areas.

Since no public funds were available from the School Board to start this latest offshoot of the Parkway, Mrs. Rasmussen got some grant money from the Philadelphia Foundation to get going with the help of eighteen volunteer teachers.

The 150 children (aged five to ten years) who attend this center get free medical care and home-cooked meals. One disadvantaged mother of seven children (all under age nine), who had four of them attending the Center, found out that she enjoyed going to the Center herself. "It's like going from my little house to my bigger house," she said proudly.

Mrs. Rasmussen, a refugee from Hitler's Nazi Germany and a mother of three teenage sons, feels that her quiet revolutionary approach to innovation at the elementary Durham Center will

142

provide greater dividends later on than her better publicized secondary rival over on the Parkway. "Our publicity can come later after we are successful," she says.

The Durham Center along with the Parkway Program are only two of the more prominent educational innovations that abound in the Philadelphia city school system. Most of the other seven learning centers, like the Durham Center, specialize in the area of early childhood education which marks a revolutionary approach to education stemming "from the bottom up" as Lore Rasmussen so eloquently put it.

A firm believer that "there is no one Mecca or one Moses" to lead us out of the educational bulrushes, Mrs. Rasmussen is firmly rooted to a humane approach to educating children in a pattern built upon Parkway foundations with her own ideas attached. Her main contribution is the realization that the family can be educated together, with the parents and children learning jointly in a voluntary consortium. This concept expands the confines of education beyond the classroom to the home and the community at large.

In her report to the parents at the end of the first year at the Durham Center, Mrs. Gloria Bush, the head of the kindergarten through fourth grade Learning Center, gave her analysis of the growth and development of the Center in an essay entitled "A Climate of Trust." In this report, Mrs. Bush stressed the fact that the teachers at the Center received far more from the children than they gave out; that what was really happening at Durham was the "touching of young humans, of awakening children to the unlimited possibilities of learning."

She went on to say that the classroom atmosphere at the DLC required a special "climate" to enhance the growth of the children. This situation is created by an arrangement called the "free" school day or integrated day, in which the children's learning day is not divided up into segments called subject names, i.e., spelling, handwriting, social studies, etc. Mrs. Bush concluded:

"We have proceeded cautiously in fully opening some classrooms, often in the face of parental urgings that we speed the process. A wider use of the resources within the Center itself seems to be the next step toward freeing the children to pursue their interests and curiosities. We have made a slow but steady beginning in the use of the broader learning environment—the

Philadelphia community and its environs. To stop our use of our surroundings even at that stage would be to slam shut the doors of knowledge to the children.

"We consider, ideally, the total learning environment of your child to be nothing less than the universe itself. We try to interpret that idea, even to our youngest children. For to be educated is to be prepared to understand one's own role in the universe as a person with rights, but with the capability and responsibility of being a world-changer. . . .

"The universe as a learning site seems to be too huge and complex to be fully examined, probed, interpreted, and understood. The small interlinked community of the Durham Center is not. Its organization, function, population, and services are clearly relevant to the larger community the children will inherit."

Under Buttenwieser's and Rasmussen's inspired leadership, the Durham Learning Center has evolved into one big happy family. Parents go to school at the same time as their children and in some cases learn together in the same classroom; whether it is the day-care center, the arts and crafts room, the basement plywood and cardboard game room, which was constructed by students, or the other converted formerly elementary classrooms. Many of these rooms are hardly recognizable. Gone are the former stiff rows of seats and desks and in their place are informally grouped chairs and tables.

"There is a new, heady atmosphere here," said one of the DLC teachers proudly. "We are quietly witnessing the wave of the future in education and are actually previewing what the schools of tomorrow may look like."

SOME INTANGIBLE SPIN-OFFS

The Parkway's Impact in the Delaware Valley

Dr. Shedd envisions the new Parkway wall-less educational institution as a "kind of school that might really prove to the suburbs what Philadelphia can offer." He sees the potential high-quality program of the project resulting in a "richness of an offering that no one single school can afford."

One of the other possible spin-offs of this infant educational experiment is the two-way benefit to both the students and the

144

Parkway class viewing Danish flying-saucer home.

cooperating institutions involved. It was felt that each could bring worthwhile innovative learning approaches to the other. Robert Neathery, a vice-president of the Franklin Institute and head of its Science Museum Education Department for the past twenty-five years, sees the Parkway school's utilization of the institute's educational and scientific facilities as a challenge.

"There are at least two good things readily apparent about the Program," he said candidly while awaiting the first experimental class of ninth graders to descend upon him. "First, the students can work at their own pace in small sections, and secondly, there are no restrictions in regard to curriculum content; rather the learning areas to be explored will be governed by what the youngsters want to learn."

Dr. Shedd believes that the concept of the school without walls is a "powerful one" along with the West Philadelphia Community Free School idea which has recently come to life. "We need both alternatives," he said, "to supplement the public school. The community based mini-school will permit great divergence from the present fixed structure."

He felt that the City Hall opposition to both educational ideas would "have an ultimate effect on the rest of the school program, since one has to expect such opposition when one is dealing with innovative and controversial programs like the Parkway and the Free School ideas."

In the long run, however, the intangible impact of the Parkway Program may be of more lasting benefit than the tangible ones of operating a school without walls. Such intangible spin-offs as improved relations with suburban educational systems, shaking up the cooperating cultural institutions by helping them to freshen up their dusty, moss-backed atmospheres, and bringing new vitality to a decadent city and its educational system are definitely some of these aftereffects to watch in the future.

Sometimes the little observed and underappreciated intangibles are more significant than the tangibles. In the case of the Parkway Program, this judgment could prove to be the correct one.

Schools Without Walls in Gotham City

In March, 1971, Dr. Harvey Scribner, the new Chancellor of the New York City public schools, announced to his board and the community that new educational methods under study in the nation's largest city ranged from greater use of the informal, open classroom on the elementary school level to independent, off school premises programs of study for high school students.

Both of these concepts were adaptions of the Philadelphia Parkway Program. The amazing thing about this announcement was the length of time that it took for the school without walls idea to trickle one hundred miles northward considering the rapidity of the modern communications media in transmitting information these days. In retrospect, two years may seem to be a short time today as compared with the generation length period that it formerly took to adapt a valid educational program in other states and school systems in the past.

Two months earlier, the School Community Committee of Public School 116 in Manhattan had quietly unveiled a detailed proposal for a first, daring school without walls in New York. This committee, which included parents, teachers, and administrators, represented a school that is 50 percent Spanish-speaking; 35 percent "other," meaning middle-class white; 10 percent black; and 5 percent Oriental. [3]

Their proposal, which was carefully researched, relied heavily on the Parkway Program in Philadelphia. It called for seeking the motivation for learning outside the confines of the multiracial school. The Public School 116 Committee report read in part:

> There are a great many children who, having reached the fifth and sixth grades, cannot read up to their grade level in spite of great efforts to teach them. Their interest in school is minimal, and their failures are bound to be perpetuated in secondary school. They become the dropouts, the unskilled workers, and the social problems.[4]

The committee felt that for those children, who now fail, nothing will change until the schools make use of "the total environment" and let children see themselves as active participants—and incidentally learners—in their community.

Although their plan was similar to the Philadelphia approach in many ways, it went a step further by placing greater reliance on the school itself, calling for a special curriculum to be worked out in detail by the school's staff, together with professionals, workers, and other experts in the community. Part of the stu-

[3] *The New York Times,* January 18, 1970, p. E 11.
[4] *Ibid.*

dent's experience would be to find out how adults fill out job applications—and to discover their need of basic writing and reading skills.

Children under the New York scheme would become, like their counterparts in the City of Brotherly Love, not only students of their community, but also active participants in many community actions as well. Specifically, they were to learn how a house was built, how an apartment was furnished, what sorts of jobs were involved, and what the rewards of labor might be.

They would also learn about the running of mass transportation, hospitals, police stations, and post offices. These community experiences would be reinforced with formal learning that would help these students to unlock the mysteries of life and to find out what makes their community tick.

In order to succeed, the planners from this elementary middle school felt that the out-of-school program would have to start at age three and continue through the eighth grade. Thus, there would have to be a day-care center for children of working parents, and provision for some children to spend a much longer day in school. Many of the lessons and explorations would be shared by children and parents.

Besides borrowing from the Parkway concept, the Public School 116 (PS 116) plan also lifted some ideas from the Deweyesque "learn by doing" concept of the twenties, but with greater recognition of the need to plan carefully and not to neglect the formal aspects of learning.

The combination of the school's fuller involvement with the child's growing up and the more frequent participation of the parents in the learning process went a step beyond the Parkway with the inclusion of ideas borrowed from the Scandinavian educational experiences and the collective settlements of the Israeli kibbutzim.

The PS 116 committee realized that they couldn't translate their plan into action overnight, that about two years of preparation would be essential. This planning time compared favorably with the similar incubation period of the Parkway Program. The New York group understood that to bring about the working cooperation of lay people and professionals on one side, and between the school and community on the other, would require a greater degree of risk taking than was to be found in most

148

communities. Another semi-Parkway type of high school experiment in New York is Harlem Prep, a unique school which has recently been set up specifically for urban dropouts. Harlem Prep was established just prior to the Parkway (in October, 1967), and in its first three years it produced 214 graduates, all but 10 of whom were still attending colleges somewhere in the United States by May, 1971.

This school is an open-spaced building that was formerly a supermarket. The students, mostly black and Puerto Rican, are all between the ages of seventeen and twenty-one. They came from the streets of New York and turned their school into an extension of the streets, transforming it into an arena for open discussion of their choice of subjects, teachers, and rules of decorum. "This is part of the revolution," said one Harlem Prep student proudly.

As a vital educational institution, the immediacy of classroom discussions ranged from black history to the meaning of the modern classic *The Stranger* by Albert Camus. One young student, looking out over the slums of Harlem, explained that he didn't want to change the people, rather "I just want to change those buildings, that's all."

Their graduation ceremonies took place in the middle of a Harlem street, with the sound of fire engines punctuating the solemnity of the singing of the class hymn, "To Be Young, Gifted, and Black." As one of the foremost educational alternatives in the country, along with the Parkway Program, this variation of the "open classroom" concept bears watching in the future.

New York was not the only other large city to give serious thought to adopting a Parkway experiment in its environs. Some cities in the hinterlands experimented with the idea even earlier.

The Parkway Comes to the Midwest

A year after the opening of Philadelphia's school without walls, some bright students in Milwaukee, Wisconsin, who believed that much of their high school experience had been a waste of time, quietly dropped out of their old public and private schools to form the Milwaukee Independent School. This new institution, modeled closely after the Parkway experiment, was built around the concept of each student choosing what he wants to study, how he wants to study it, and where he will do his learning.

This latest novel educational innovation got underway during the second week of February, 1970, when thirty-five Milwaukee teenagers, who were among the most successful students in the best high schools in the city, got together to form their avant garde M.I.S., as they called their new school for short. This reform-oriented educational institution was established as a meaningful alternative to the conventional schools.

They envisioned their action as a peaceful revolt in the democratic tradition against the oppressive characteristics of secondary education as it has been recently practiced in the United States.

"Too many things are done in school only for the school's purposes and not the students," says Bill Ahlhauser, who maintained a 95 average when he attended Marquette High, a prestigious Jesuit parochial [secondary] school.

"There is an extreme lack of respect for students in many schools. Students' initiative and creativity are impeded and inhibited. It [school] is terribly dull, and the kids are pitted against each other for grades and rank in class."

His criticism was seconded by pretty Belinda Behne, a slim animated 17-year-old, who had made straight A's and B's at John Marshall High School, which is generally regarded as one of Milwaukee's best. "Kids are pumped through the system like products, never learning to think at all," she said.

Jim Boulet, eighteen, who formerly was enrolled at Riverside High, described his life there as a first semester senior this way: "Here was this nice sterile little cubicle, and you'd turn your mind off when you went inside. When you got out, you'd turn it back on. What went on in the classroom had nothing to do with the world, and they called this learning."

The new M.I.S. was based on the basic premises "that all students have serious personal interests; that these interests should be the starting point for education; that they should be developed and enriched by firsthand contact with human life; and that the function of reading, writing and formal academic inquiry is to facilitate the process." [5]

[5] Quotes regarding M.I.S. are from William K. Stevens, "Students in Milwaukee Form Their Own School," *The New York Times,* February 13, 1970, p. L 34.

These students agreed that learning never stops and that it goes on outside of school. Consequently, they planned to spend only a relatively small portion of their time in the somewhat dilapidated white frame building which serves as a library, discussion hall, and home base.

They spent most of the first week in February painting and plastering the inside of the building and planning their new curriculum. They proposed to enter into their studies under the wing of a qualified adult volunteer from the community who might be a biochemist, an engineer, or someone from the business world.

When the grapevine word got around in Milwaukee that the new school was about to open, some eighty students applied for the limited thirty-five places available. The final thirty-five were chosen by lot. All but two (who were black) were the sons and daughters of white middle-class families. Some of these students knew in advance what studies they wished to pursue, but others, like their predecessors on the Parkway, knew that there would be difficult moments adjusting to the nonauthoritarian, nonrigid arrangement that pervaded the new M.I.S.

One thing appeared fairly certain and that was the prospect that, once launched, few of the students would leave to go back to the old conventional system.

Some of the Milwaukee students planned to obtain part-time jobs while others planned to live for brief periods in specialized settings. Jim Boulet, for example, who wished to study religion with a possible career in this field in mind, planned to live in a monastery, then with a rabbi, and finally with a minister—so he could get the feel of all three major American faiths.

All the students planned to undertake individual research projects tied to their own interests. Special attention was to be placed on the development of basic communications skills— within a purposive context, such as analytical reading, invective writing, and coherent speech—instead of the bland approach to these skills practiced by the typical high school teachers.

These eager students were aided in their neophyte experiment with the help of Paul H. Krueger, who left his post as Professor of Education at the University of Wisconsin's Milwaukee campus to become a full-time coordinator of the new school. His meager salary was paid for by community donations, starting with an initial pot of $4500. The students felt that a goal of $40,000 was needed to get their enterprise on firm ground. Fortunately, most parents and students involved greeted the new experiment with a mixture of more enthusiasm than foreboding, although they all recognized the major problems facing them in their gamble. [6]

One immediate problem was the question of whether they were to be declared absent under the state's compulsory school attendance laws until their new school could be declared a bonafide educational institution. This dilemma brought to light another unanswered educational question: Just which local or state authority has the right to give such an approval?

This impasse, which has cropped up in other states, such as New York, Pennsylvania, California, and Washington, where parents have pulled their children out of the regular conventional schools, has raised a fundamental question in American education (which fortunately did not undermine the Parkway Program in its early days). The question is:

Who should determine what education is?

The students in Milwaukee's M.I.S. believed that they themselves should determine the answer to this question. They believed that what went on in their former schools was, for the most part, not education. They pointed out the negative features of conventional education including the emphasis on pleasing and outguessing the teacher rather than on discovering, thinking, and exploring; the almost total divorce of school work from reality as perceived by the students in the world around them; and finally too much of an over-reliance on grades.

These same views were shared by the Parkway students when they were quizzed about their criticisms of their former schools. Their criticisms also paralleled those voiced by activist high school students in other parts of the country.

Significantly, the Milwaukee students wrote to colleges to find out if their enrollment in the M.I.S. would adversely affect their chances of admission when they completed their secondary schooling. Many, including Harvard University, replied that it would have no adverse effect. Fordham University wrote back that conversely, attendance at the M.I.S. would even enhance the students' chances. Most students felt confident that they would have

[6] *Ibid.*

no trouble in passing the standardized college entrance tests when their time came to take them.

Milwaukee and New York were only two of the more prominent cities following in the vanguard of Philadelphia's lead in establishing a secondary school without walls. In February, 1971, Chicago took the plunge, by starting its own Chicago Metro High School, modeled after the Parkway.

If this concept could work on the high school level, why not on the university level also? The idea has already taken root in higher educational circles.

And Now—Colleges Without Walls

The pioneer higher educational institution without walls is the Friends World College located in Westbury, Long Island, on the site of an old millionaire's estate. This unique college is the first true world university—since the whole of the planet Earth is its campus. The Friends World College was established by the Society of Friends to incorporate the Quaker tradition of direct learning experiences for its student body.

Although it was technically founded in 1958, the first experimental program involving twenty-two students who represented countries from Africa, Asia, Europe, Latin America, and North America did not get started until the summer of 1963. The faculty came from over a half dozen different countries and was under the guidance of its first director, Dr. Morris Mitchell.

The students were encouraged to live and travel around the world, working out of one or the other of the seven major decentralized centers set up by this college without national boundaries. In May, 1968, the Quaker institution became fully accredited when it received a provisional five-year charter from the Regents of the University of the State of New York.

The first thirty-eight North American students who enrolled at the Friends World College Mitchell Gardens' campus at Westbury in September, 1965, spent their first semester in Mexico, moved on to Europe for their 1966-67 academic year, and then to Africa and India in 1967-68.

Using the whole world as a cultural and educational center for the first time, FWC has proved the practicality of the Parkway-like program on an international basis. The FWC has been the *only* case in America of a school without walls actually preceding the Parkway. But in terms of its operational status, however, it is different in that its level of learning is restricted to post-high school age groups.

Actually, the idea for a world university was first put forward over fifty years ago in the League of Nations at Geneva where it was suggested that a new type of university be established to take in the world's scholars and students as its community. The FWC has incorporated some of this old idea into its operations and program. To the FWC, the world is a schoolhouse.

The authorities at the college are more interested in the student's personal qualifications and interests than in his past academic achievements in high school. So far, the student body has been limited mainly to affluent whites, who can afford the high costs of travel and tuition, although a few limited scholarships for members of minority groups are available at this private, nonprofit institution.

A typical four-year FWC student will spend at least three and one-half years abroad and the remainder back on the home campus in Long Island writing a thesis on his or her experiences. The tuition of this college, $2000 per year, is much lower, however, than most Ivy League universities.

Once they get to a foreign country of their choice, most of the students are taught to accept the responsibility for making their own local living arrangements, instead of falling back on the college to do this for them.

There are no exams, no entrance requirements, and no grades at the FWC. The first graduating class of sixteen in 1970, was called the "Survivors" rather than the traditional "Seniors." These students were able to "survive" by narrowing their focus to special interests of their own choosing. Although the dropout rate is high (only twelve of the first forty students graduated), the FWC is already considered a success, despite financial burdens.

The philosophy behind the global curriculum of the FWC, like that of the Parkway, is a radical one. It is based on a series of practical judgments by its founders and Quaker board members that the life most of us live is not as good as it could be and is not improving for most people. Utilizing the assumption that the educational system has some bearing on the quality of one's life and is presently intended to perpetuate existing values, the FWC

154

planners agreed that present trends suggest the system will continue to do so as long as it is structured along rigid departmental, campus-restricting lines. The FWC students and faculty therefore believe in attempting to change our value system by getting out into the world and establishing a new approach to learning.

They have decided that the traditional structure of the university with walls precludes and inhibits any significant change in our ethical outlook on ourselves. In order to bring about meaningful change, one has to put oneself in the others' shoes. To accomplish this end, the Quakers, following their quiet, practical, nonviolent tradition, put together a new higher educational pattern instead of trying to tear down the existing structures of higher learning.

The Friends World College is not the only case of a college without walls in the upper levels of learning. More recently, some other proposals to establish similar institutions on a local or regional basis have been put forth for consideration.

Although it is not a direct spin-off of the Parkway, the publication of the report "A College in the City: An Alternative," by the Educational Facilities Laboratories (EFL) branch of the Ford Foundation in early 1969 represented one of the first examples of an extension of the school-without-walls concept to a post-high school level institution of learning.

This study, which appeared at the same time that the Parkway Program became operational, was headed by Dr. William Birenbaum, the President of Staten Island Community College. It offered a promising new way of looking at the university in the city, by utilizing the ghetto land of Brooklyn's Bedford-Stuyvesant section as a campus for a theoretical college without walls.

The report suggests that urban universities might benefit by breaking out from the confines of their ivy-covered walls and at the same time aid in the restoration of blighted parts of our inner cities.

The college-in-the-city plan envisions the utilization of old, abandoned brownstone houses, tenements, factories, and storefronts as classrooms for a community of 500,000 that is 95 percent Negro or Puerto Rican. Many of these poor people have no opportunity at present to go on to college, even to the so-called open enrollment branches of the City College of New York.

Helping to restore the run-down sections of the Bedford-Stuyvesant section by converting old row houses into college classrooms could go a long way toward reversing the present trend toward deterioration in this core city within a city, according to the writers of the EFL report.

Scattered community facilities which were available for potential use by this still unborn wall-less college were a local armory, a fire station, a hospital and nursing home, a high school, a library, a post office, parks, vacant lots, housing projects, and other similar locales.

The resulting mixed occupancy of buildings, staggered along main 'arterial thoroughfares, i.e., urban residential housing next to a decentralized classroom building, which might be removed from its nearest sister classroom in the wider city campus by several blocks, had several distinct advantages over the traditional isolated, walled-in campus.

The multiple use of these buildings, with stores on the ground floor, possible classrooms on the second, and walk-up apartments on the upper floors lends an air of community integration that retains the fabric of the social pattern of the neighborhoods without destroying it or drastically altering it.

Furthermore, the ideas of an urban mix-and-joint occupancy could give the college a better chance to help the community through its difficult periods of change since it would be a part of the community, not an outsider. Although a concrete plan has not yet been brought forth to implement this concept in Brooklyn, its philosophy is applicable in any large city or university.

In late December, 1970, the United States Office of Education made a $415,000 planning grant to seventeen established colleges to allow a limited number of students, ranging in age from sixteen to sixty, to conduct an experiment in a university without walls. These colleges agreed to allow the selected students to work toward their degrees without any of the fixed requirements on any one campus.

Although most students would be expected to take some of their academic work as regular campus residents wherever they were enrolled, with the right to switch at will to any one of the cooperating institutions, most of their work would be done off campus, utilizing the same type of local cultural institutions as had Philadelphia's Parkway Program.

A handful of college students started this senior Parkway-type

156

effort in February, 1971, but full-scale operations with from seventy-five to one hundred students at each of the cooperating colleges was not slated to begin until the fall semester of 1971.

Some of the schools which agreed to cooperate in the University-Without-Walls Project were the University of Minnesota, Antioch College, Shaw University, Howard University, Illinois State College, Goddard College, the University of South Carolina, and Staten Island Community College. The latter institution was presided over by the same Dr. William Birenbaum who chaired the Ford Foundation's "A College in the City" project discussed earlier.

The USOE planners envision that a typical cross section of students who would take advantage of this new innovative program would be middle-aged housewives, army veterans without previous college experience, and frustrated undergraduates who were seeking a transfer without loss of credits.

Not to be upstaged by the U.S. Office of Education, the Ford Foundation and the Carnegie Corporation announced a similar grant program two months later in February, 1971, to help start two new off-campus degree programs in higher education in the state of New York.[7] A $1.8 million award to the State University of New York and the State Education Department was made to set up a similar pattern to the University of London's external degree program and Britain's new Open University. This program which could bring about a further radical change in higher education in America also owed much of its inception to the Parkway Program. An estimated five hundred adult students were expected to take advantage of this new program in 1971-72.

At the same time, the Ford Foundation also announced an additional $400,000 grant to nineteen institutions participating in the planning and development of the new University-Without-Walls program. A third grant of $300,000 was made by Ford to the Policy Institute of Syracuse University to establish an external baccalaureate degree program coordinated through local institutions in five neighboring counties. [8]

Dr. Samuel Baskin, a psychology professor from Antioch College, was the driving force behind this unique project. Undoubt-

[7] See M. S. Handler, "$1.8 Million to Aid Off-Campus Studies," *The New York Times*, Feb. 17, 1971, p. 1.
[8] *Ibid.*, p. 33.

157

edly he had heard of the success of the Antioch interns who had been working in the Parkway Program for the past two years. He also served as president of a new organization called the Union of Experimenting Colleges and Universities, of which the University Without Walls was one of his first models.

Baskin borrowed from John Dewey's "learn by doing" philosophy as well as from the Parkway Program concept to mold his project to the point where the government was willing to fund what only the Ford Foundation had been willing to gamble on previously.

He realized that he would have problems, i.e., recruiting adjunct professors from local business and government enterprises, overcoming the resistance of traditional academic departments, adjusting to the new learning technologies of TV, cassettes, computers, and the four years on campus syndrome.

But Baskin was optimistic in believing that despite these risks involved, the majority of the students would exert the maturity, independence, and integrity to make the project function well. He foresaw that the freewheeling minority of college students could be freed from the confining structure surrounding the majority of students who felt more secure if their college programs were mapped out for them in advance. Ultimately, he felt this new "Parkway" university could even soften the mold of tradition for the majority and free them in the process.

Closely akin to the concept of a college-without-walls idea— whether it be located in the city, or in a small town—was the gist of a report made by the Newman Committee to the Nixon Administration in March, 1971, challenging the traditional institutions of higher education and calling for the development of an alternative system. This report, one and one-half years in the making, was the result of a study group chaired by Frank Newman, the Associate Director of University Relations at Stanford University, and performed under the instigation of former Secretary of Health, Education and Welfare, Robert Finch.

This Ford Foundation-sponsored study recommended among other changes that new forms of off-campus education be developed and that academic credit and even degrees be granted for experiences derived outside the classroom. It also suggested the development of informal tutors from whom persons could obtain academic assistance. All these specific concepts were pioneered

158

first by the Parkway Program, which shows how one Ford-funded educational idea can borrow practical innovations from another, with the added advantage of utilizing those concepts that have proved their worth in the fire of experience and discarding the rest.

The Newman Report also pointed out that both faculty and students in most present-day colleges live in an isolated community that bears little resemblance to the real world. It doubted whether education could be made more relevant to students and society simply by developing new curricula because it said too few students and faculty members have enough experience outside the present educational system to know what is relevant.

Maybe some colleges could use a seminar chaired by some Parkway students or alumni to show them what is "relevant" in the real world.

A forerunner of this new type of college education is that of the thirty Columbia University juniors and seniors who devoted the entire spring semester of 1971 to a single course in political science worth fifteen points. This unique experimental course was conceived by forty-one-year-old Dr. Alan Westin, who not only is a political-science professor but also is a specialist in teaching techniques. It evolved out of Westin's concern following the 1968 student riots and political crisis at Columbia which he felt had educational overtones.

He knew that "many students were tired and uncomfortable with the standard lecture-type course" and so he proceeded to prepare a course called "The Seminar Institute on American Politics and Social Change," where some students stay in class up to thirteen hours a day in what they consider a "constructive revolution" in education. [9]

What was the course all about? During the first phase of the course, the students discussed particular political-social events like the recent Ocean Hill-Brownsville education controversy that aroused national attention. The seven middle weeks of the course were spent in individual field research and writing outside of the college, interviewing people who stood on both sides of the issue in their own habitats. The final four weeks were spent in evalu-

[9] Alan Westin, "Civic Education in a Crisis Age," mimeographed paper sponsored by Ford and Danforth Foundations and presented at Conference on the School and the Democratic Environment, April 10, 1969.

159

ation and rewriting. The pattern of this course, except for its all-day aspects, resembled many of the Parkway courses.

A Bridge from a School with to a School Without Walls

Many present public school teachers would like to make better use of the resources of their local communities to expand learning within the present four confining walls of their classrooms, but they seldom know how to locate such resources. As a stepping stone to a full-fledged school without walls in their own community, there is much that a teacher can do to prepare the way.

Two cities, Teaneck, New Jersey, and Minneapolis, Minnesota, have recently set up central offices to channel community people and services into the existing schools. Teaneck's Operation Community Talent and Minneapolis's Community Resource Volunteers each maintain extensive and expanding files on local parents, businessmen, and professional people who have volunteered to fill teachers' requests for classroom speakers, field trips, films, and tutorial help in their respective specialized areas of expertise.

Teaneck's referral agency serves kindergarten through high school while Minneapolis's clearinghouse works only with elementary schools at present. To use this service in Teaneck, a teacher need only fill out a simple form or telephone in a request. OCT's two-man staff then locates the appropriate resource. Minneapolis supplies guidebooks to each elementary school from which teachers select speakers by subject. CRV then makes all the specific arrangements. Both of these agencies then evaluate each volunteer's performance for future use in a follow-up operation. Originally begun under a Title III grant of the Elementary and Secondary Education Act of 1965, these agencies are now both funded by local school boards.

Volunteers enrich schoolroom learning in many ways, in every conceivable subject. Textbook social studies come alive through conversation with a foreign visitor. In one class in Teaneck, the study of the human eye concluded with the visit of a blind teen-ager with her Seeing-Eye dog. As adults participate in the classroom, occupational problems become real and hobbies interesting. The children in these communities imitate their Parkway counterparts by visiting local hospitals, courthouses, an artist's studio, and local historical sites.

160

OCT in Teaneck makes a special effort to involve people of all ages. Senior citizens share local history and high school students do tutoring. Local doctors discuss the human body while a lawyer defines justice and how it works. Not only do teachers and classes benefit, but the community develops a closer relationship with the schools and accepts responsibility beyond paying bills.

Many community residents are willing to participate in the educational experience under official auspices, if they can be made available in other communities. Agencies such as those now operating in Teaneck and Minneapolis may become a transitional stage between a four-walled school and a wall-less school. Any community willing to gamble and designate one full-time person to staff a similar office may achieve comparable benefits.

Spreading the Seed

The eight different types of direct and indirect Parkway-spawned offshoots that have been discussed in the foregoing pages are like the seedlings from a tree taking root elsewhere. Their life span, like that of the parent, depends upon the careful nourishment given the roots of the young trees as they mature and grow. The examples pointed out in this chapter prove conclusively that the Parkway concept can be extended both upward and downward so as to encompass all levels of education. The idea of a school without walls is not restricted to just the secondary level.

The pioneer Parkway Program has set the pace as an educational first and those offshoots that follow in its footsteps can profit by its successes and failures in the years to come.

13. Does the Parkway Program Have a Future?

"America has never had an educational system worthy of itself."   *John Bremer*

What is wrong with most high school education in America today is that its general repression of students has taken on the subtle overtones of an educational Vietnamization of our youth. This subconscious goal is coupled with a lack of a clearly defined purpose compounded by an overemphasis on architectural school building sex appeal as a first priority. While many of our modern high school edifices look good to the roving eye, both from an exterior and interior point of view, their curricula usually fail to focus on humanness and the joy of learning.

The free-swinging Parkway Program presents a sharp contrast to these modern mausoleums of mindlessness and is already serving as a contemporary beacon for the new learning of tomorrow that will accentuate the attributes of the human spirit that are missing in today's academic factories. The school-without-walls concept has successfully broken the iron grip of the assembly-line learning routine that has undermined the educational process.

Silberman pinpointed this need when he concluded in his *Crisis in the Classroom* that our most pressing educational problem is not how to increase the efficiency of the schools; it is how to create and maintain a humane society. A society whose schools are inhumane is not likely to be humane itself. [1] The Parkway Program has unconsciously and consciously aimed its sights at

[1] Charles E. Silberman, *Crisis in the Classroom* (New York: Random House, Inc., 1970), p. 524.

helping to transform a sick society by setting itself up as a humanitarian honeycomb so that other educational institutions can eventually be drawn to its bosom.

Before he left, Bremer had a vision of the need to politicize the Parkway student body whereby each pupil became his own motivational creator to help transform the blighted city around him into a more livable place. This goal, in the long run, may even become the primary legacy of the Parkway educational effort.

Despite his vacillations during the early period of the Parkway Program, Mark Shedd became firmly committed to the effort, even more forcefully than during the hectic days of the Bremer regime. "There are people in the system who don't want it," he admitted confidentially, "and think it's a waste of money. They say, 'Why are you spending money on this?' [But] I think absolutely it's worth the money. We must commit ourselves to developing alternatives within the system." [2]

Paul Goodman, the noted American educational critic and author of *The New Reformation* and other works, partly disagreed with Shedd that the Parkway can best work within the system. He recently expressed the view after a visit to Philadelphia that "the only way for the Parkway Program to work properly is to divorce itself from the confining shackles of the school board and branch out on its own as an independent entity." [3] Whether such a drastic move can be achieved without sacrificing the present public-supported foundations of the program is debatable.

While it still remains as a part of the system, however, the Parkway Program has already proved itself as a healthy antidote to help counteract some of the more flagrant happenings in the Philadelphia schools. The increasing drug traffic within the regular schools has not taken a similar toll on the Parkway. The smaller classes, combined with the fact that the students are rarely bored or apathetic, have worked to the advantage of the Parkway Program in keeping its drug abuse incidents to an infinitesimally low figure. [4] This is the reverse of the situation found in many of the regular high schools where the students look upon

[2] As quoted by Nancy Love, "Grooving at Parkway," *Philadelphia Magazine,* June, 1970, p. 126.

[3] Interview with author, Philadelphia education seminar, Nov., 1970.

[4] Statistics provided by Dr. Bremer in a personal interview with author, January, 1970.

drug addiction as a game that they play with the school authorities to escape the boredom of their institutions.

Many observers of our present system of public education—
with its coercive methods—view its unsatisfactory end-products
as a symptom of the deterioration of our democratic way of life.
At the same time our inability to reorder our priorities both at
home and abroad in a rational manner may well stem directly
from the breakdown in our educational process. The normal,
healthy growth of our typical school children has been nicotinized
in every city and town of America.

A frustrated Dr. Shedd confessed to this disillusioning fact in
January, 1971, some three and one-half years after he had become
superintendent of schools in Philadelphia. For the first time during
his stormy tenure, the usually flaccid Shedd confessed publicly that
most of the local public school students were still not receiving
a "good education."

Instead, this leader of the modern reform movement in urban
educational administration, who had pledged himself to help turn
Philadelphia's school system into the "best in the U.S." by 1972,
found himself supervising a sinking academic ship that verged
on bankruptcy. Furthermore, he presided over the first teachers'
strike in the city's history in September, 1970, and faced the prospect of a complete shutdown of the schools before the end of
1971 due to a lack of money to pay his staff and running expenses.

By early 1971, Shedd reluctantly had to revise his earlier
thoughts concerning the length of time it would take to improve
the sick system which he inherited. After struggling with a myriad
of complex problems to patch up the system since September,
1967, Shedd came to believe that it would take another ten to fifteen years to revamp the system adequately.

Meanwhile, Shedd continued to defend the Parkway Program
from the constant carping of its critics, the local politicians and
school people, who wished to see it either buried or compromised.
He still found time to say an occasional kind word for the school
without walls as criticism began to shift to the weaknesses in the
instructional and disciplinary programs of the rest of the system.
By late 1970 and early 1971, ugly racial disturbances had erupted
in several large city high schools. Fortunately, the Parkway complex remained immune to these episodes.

Violence in the Philadelphia schools reached a peak in February, 1971, when Samson Freedman, a bearded, white, manual-training teacher at Leeds Junior High School, was shot and killed on the school grounds by a fourteen-year-old black student. In the wake of this tragic incident, the Philadelphia Federation of Teachers asked for and received permission from the beleaguered administration to close the schools the next day as a dual symbol of mourning and protest over the loss of their colleague.

In the aftermath of this murder, Shedd, the Philadelphia public school principals, and the Board came under great public and parental pressure to impose a new "get tough" policy on the students. Shedd reacted by presenting the Board with a 12-point disciplinary plan a few weeks later which stopped just short of putting all the city schools, including the Parkway, under armed police rule and the institution of corporal punishment for wayward students.

The Board of Education itself was divided over the issue. At a public meeting of the Board, the majority of the audience cheered proposals to allow corporal punishment in the schools. A few of the speakers, including the head of the principals' association, urged caution.

But these fervent pleas for sanity fell largely on deaf ears as most of the parents present signified their endorsement of the harsh proposals which they hoped would improve both discipline and learning in the public schools. Ironically enough, none of the speakers (at this meeting or a follow-up one held two weeks later) offered any humane constructive alternatives to solving the problem nor did they help the Board to examine the root causes of the ferment in the schools. The "why" factor was ignored almost completely at these emotional meetings.

The main weakness of these meetings was that symptoms and solutions to the discipline problem were put forth without an in-depth examination of the causes of the rash of incidents that triggered them. This new wave of hysteria that swept the Philadelphia school system and the community in early 1971 signified a regression back to the dark ages of the nineteenth century in American education practices when teachers on the frontier were given the right to use the rod as they saw fit.

The attempts to impose corporal punishment on school children seemed to symbolize a breakdown in communications between the school, society, and the home, with a group of frightened parents, school administrators, and board members seeking an easy out from a complex problem. The tragedy of this situation was the naïve belief that everything would return to normal once repressive measures were put on the books so that the students could be returned to their "rightful place." [5]

A further ugly sign of the deterioration of the local citizens' faith in the future of the Philadelphia public schools appeared when the City Council voted by an overwhelming 14 to 1 margin to pass an ordinance on March 11, 1971, prohibiting any "unauthorized persons" from entering the local public schools. Such "unauthorized" people would include even parents or any adult visitor unless they had a special permission to visit the school in advance.

The harsh penalty for breaking this oppressive law was a $300 fine and imprisonment for up to ninety days. Only a single councilman, one of the three blacks, had the courage to vote against this act that would literally convert the public schools into walled fortresses. He voted "No" on the grounds that the law was both "unconstitutional" and a breach of the citizens' right to "peacefully demonstrate in the city's public schools." But he was shouted down by those who fearfully felt that most of the trouble in the schools was essentially caused by the outsiders. This panic legislation, rushed through City Council without an adequate hearing, reflected the growing atmosphere of fear that pervaded the community. It also served as an indirect threat to the viability and survival of the Parkway Program, since the philosophy of the school without walls represented the very antithesis of the intent of the legislation. City Council wanted *closed* schools. The Parkway stood for the *open* school idea.

The Parkway Program cried out against this backward trend and continued to struggle as a meaningful alternative to the largely irrelevant public schools. It was obvious that the emerging police-state, public school policy of the Board and the city government would have a significant impact on the future health of the Parkway Program. City Council failed utterly to take into consideration how their poorly thought-out piece of legislation might apply to the Parkway institution.

[5] On March 29, 1971, the Philadelphia School Board voted to approve corporal punishment (paddling of students by teachers) for all "disruptive" children in grades one to eight. The vote was 4-3.

For instance, how does a stranger, a parent, or a visitor go about talking with a Parkway student on the street or in a cultural institution during the school day unless that person receives prior permission to do so from the constituted school authorities? The whole idea of enforcement of this misguided act became ludicrous for both the students and administrators of Philadelphia's school without walls. Meanwhile the Parkway Program was busily grappling with more immediate problems. One factor that gave the Parkway its unique, decentralized administrative characteristic, but ultimately grew into a burden, was the lack of a single headquarters building. This concept made for an exciting variation in school administration at the start of the Program, but in practice the physical problems faced in trying to expand the Program from the crowded and noisy Alpha branch became horrendous. Therefore, Shedd and Finkelstein decided to move the director's office in the fall of 1970 to the Franklin Institute, which was conveniently located just across a side street from the school district's main headquarters.

This shift made for a more compatible relationship with the top school staff and helped to heal the rift that had grown up during Bremer's tenure of office. From his new post, Finkelstein expressed the hope that, now that he had successfully accomplished the healing of the wounds which had caused the behind-the-scenes professional estrangement, "we could now grow to a full-sized high school in the foreseeable future."

"I don't know what is the saturation point," he said cautiously, "but the downtown area could absorb another 1100 students easily."

One other possibility for expansion within the city, he pointed out, was in the new, burgeoning industrial park that was fast enveloping the vacant land surrounding the North Philadelphia Airport. "We're not locked in to any one particular type of expansion," the new director confessed, "but we may experiment with several different types. We may even consider vertical expansion as well, for a Parkway Middle School (grades 5 through 8) type of program."

This prospective future expansion downward fitted into the original pattern dreamed up by Bremer when he first took over the reins of the operation back in 1968. Furthermore, an establishment of a Parkway Middle School would probably cause less

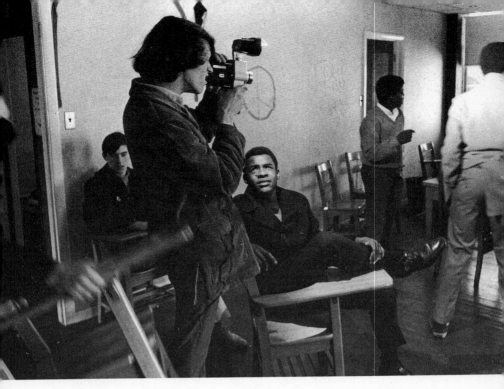

friction than the quantum jump to another elementary Paxson/
Parkway program which had upset the establishment back in late
1969.

Despite its early success, a few skeptics still believe that Philadelphia's Parkway Program will remain a unique enterprise since
it is blessed with a geographical compression of related cultural
institutions that are unrivaled by any other city in the country.
Both Brenner and Finkelstein have rejected this so-called limita-
tion by those who feel that the Parkway is not adaptable. They
came to believe that the Parkway idea was adaptable anywhere
if an urban or suburban community or complex would only set
their minds to finding ways to tailor and to fit the concept to
their area.

There were some other doubters who believed some aspects
of the Program bear watching. Silberman also wondered, and
rightly so, if the museums, newspapers, business firms, and social
service agencies would still have been willing to cooperate in
Philadelphia if a substantial majority of the city's high school
students were enrolled in the Parkway Program as Bremer ultimately envisioned. Although each cooperating institution only had

168

Experience is more
meaningful than books—
on photography
or on animal life.

to handle small groups of students for part of the work day during the first years of the Parkway's existence, one wonders how many might wish to change their minds if they suddenly were asked to handle hundreds or even thousands of students who might interfere with the completion of their regular, nine-to-five, business-oriented activities.

Despite these potential caveats, Brenner predicted confidently that "almost any large city could establish its own version of the Parkway school, even if their cultural and business institutions are not clustered in one closely knit geographical package as they are in downtown Philadelphia."

The expansion of the Parkway Program beyond the confines of Philadelphia was indirectly aided by the effective public relations efforts made by some of the staff and students as part of their extracurricular activity. Even before the first year of the Program had been completed, several volunteer bands of touring Parkway teams, made up of students, interns, and teachers, visited neighboring communities to discuss practical ways in which the school-without-walls approach might be adapted in their own backyard.

At one such assembly program held in the auditorium of Wissahickon High School in nearby Ambler during May, 1970, a group of six Parkway students, accompanied by three teachers and one intern from Antioch College, served as a panel before an appreciative afternoon audience of 650 local students, parents, and teachers. The suburban high school students asked their visitors from Philadelphia such down-to-earth questions as: "How does the Parkway system really work in practice? What type of transportation do you have to and from school? What are your classes really like?"

One of the Parkway students enlightened his listeners with a vivid description of a student-led class which helped repair Admiral George Dewey's flagship, *Olympia,* which is permanently birthed at Penn's Landing on the Delaware River. This historic antique vessel, from whose bridge Dewey shouted the famous line, "You may fire when ready, Gridley!" in the Battle of Manila Bay back in 1898, had fallen into a state of disrepair over the years.

The Parkway students obtained some surplus battleship gray paint from the local Philadelphia Naval Yard and repainted much of the vessel. They also completely refurbished the captain's cabin as part of their work-study curriculum. At the same time, they brushed up on the causes and outcomes of the Spanish-American War, which became more meaningful to them as a result of their participation in the renovation of one of the focal points of the action in that conflict.

It was obvious at the conclusion of the assembly program, that the enthusiasm of the Parkway Program's students and teachers had a positive effect on the Wissahickon student body, judging from their interest in the school-without-walls concept as shown during the discussion period.

Unfortunately, the day was partially marred by behind the scenes maneuvering of some of the Wissahickon High teachers who had tried to postpone the Parkway assembly program, since many of them felt somewhat insecure about inviting these educational mavericks from the alien turf of Philadelphia to address and proselytize their student body. But fortunately for all parties concerned, the host faculty withdrew its objections at the last minute, since the Wissahickon teachers and administrators agreed that they would be more threatened by an adverse reaction from their own students if word leaked out that they had tried to censor the opportunity for the community to acquire legitimate information concerning the operation of the school without walls.

The timing of this visit to Wissahickon High was appropriate since the local school board had recently announced that they wanted to spend an additional $16 million to erect a new high school in the vicinity to take care of the expanding student needs in the community. Many parents were complaining about the dreaded rise in taxes which would be needed to pay for the new facility. The parents in the audience that day wanted to discover for themselves, along with their sons and daughters, if an adaption of the Parkway Program was feasible in their school district for both educational and economic reasons.

When it was pointed out that the local Norristown area had few cultural institutions comparable to those on the Parkway, the delegation from Philadelphia countered with a challenge for their audience to look into the peculiar advantages of the big Fort Washington Industrial Park located nearby which could possibly serve as a locus for a local school without walls. They also encouraged their questioners to look into the possibility of using Sunday school rooms of neighboring churches that stood idle during the week.

One Parkway teacher pointed out that the best way for anyone interested in starting a Parkway-type program in his own community was to "just get in your car and drive around with your eyes open and then envision how each local facility that you pass on the road might be transformed and utilized for your own educational purposes."

When the Parkway students were asked how they adjusted to the absence of the usual sophisticated facilities found in a typical big city high school, such as adequately equipped science labs, one bright male student described how he got around this bottleneck: "I've been able to go to Temple University [in Philadelphia] where I have received permission to dissect small animals in their biology labs with the approval of both my Parkway superiors and the Temple professors."

Another Parkway student brought a laugh from the Wissahickon students when he told how a new course was put into the curriculum. "If you want a new course badly enough," he said, "and it isn't being offered, just open your mouth and you've got it. It's as simple as that." Compared with the ponderous machinations of a traditional high school bureaucracy needed to bring about any meaningful curriculum change, this response sounded like a breath of revolutionary fresh air.

In response to the high-interest question of the existence of sports activities at the Parkway, which intrigued most out-of-town students, the Parkway ambassadors agreed that they didn't miss interscholastic activities that much. "We do have swimming, hiking, and intramural basketball," said one student, "but some-day soon we'll have interleague sports activities with several near-by city high schools in most competitive sports."

The indirect payoff to the Parkway faculty and students from these unpublicized visits to suburban schools to explain the workings of their school-without-walls program was manifested in many ways. The visits provided an invaluable experience and exposure for the Parkway students to present their case in a positive way to "show-me" type audiences. They also provided good public relations opportunities, not only to promote the merits of the Parkway Program, but for the emerging metro-regional school system in the Delaware Valley. These visitations helped to overcome the antipathy fostered by certain Philadelphia and suburban school administrators and board members toward one another.

A post-Parkway assembly poll taken by the Wissahickon students showed a high degree of interest among the majority of the student body in wanting to explore further the many different options that they heretofore did not realize were possible in establishing a viable school without walls in their own community.

In time, the message of the Parkway trickled through the many local and state level educational channels and ultimately will have a long-range impact on the movers and shakers of the national educational leadership. More and more of the educational groups in the country are calling for the development of a more humane approach to education which encourages the development of each student as an individual. Since the Parkway Program is already pioneering along these lines, it is in a good position to lead a long slumbering profession out of the mossbacked academic doldrums. Beyond its immediate confines, the Parkway Program also symbolizes the strength of institutional diversity in American education. Its yeasty development emerging from a mixture of unstructured sloppiness, tradition, pragmatism, and idealism has provided a healthy response to fast changing needs.

172

The Parkway Program is actually doing more than bringing about educational change for change's sake. It is helping to bring about a rebirth of democracy that needs renewal with every generation. Without such changes aimed at providing more freedom in the schools, our educational system tends to regress into a rigid homogenization of stultifying irrelevant recipes for learning that are being constantly rammed into the minds of children in the eggbox prisons which we like to call schools.

The Parkway Program has helped to break the shackles of the prevailing educational system, which reflects the social class or ethnic composition of the community. Unlike other defacto segregated high schools found in most of our large cities and surrounding suburbs, the Parkway has practiced integration from the beginning and made it work. It has successfully given the students from the lower socioeconomic classes of Kensington and South Philadelphia a chance to compete equally with their peers from the Main Line and Chestnut Hill. This democratizing influence of the Parkway Program has not been fully appreciated by either friends or foes of the experiment.

Ronald Gross and Paul Osterman have edited a recently published book, *High School,* in which they have zeroed in on the typical American high school as "the most absurd part of an educational system pervaded by absurdity." [6] The Parkway Program has offered an escape valve from the blunting boredom of the traditional high school that Gross and Osterman have portrayed. Because it represents a learning experiment in participatory democracy, the Parkway Program has rendered a positive fertilization of its students' personalities, as contrasted with the damper effect supplied by the predominantly autocratically run public high schools.

Despite all of these advantages, the Parkway Program is not a Utopia. It has served as a preview of our educational tomorrows today, boasting a student body with a head and heart that is more fully engaged than their brethren in the older schools. Since the program gives the student a chance to operate both *on* and *in* his environment, it has to be evaluated seriously for its potential applications on not only a national but an international level.

The Parkway Program, in its two years of existence, has repre-

[6] Ronald Gross and Paul Osterman, eds., *High School* (New York: Simon & Schuster, Inc., 1971), p. 43.

sented a revolutionary force that is attempting to help bring about a much needed educational change from the straitjacket strictures of the old academic bureaucracies of the present and past. Because the Program has not grown to a monstrous, unwieldy size, it has been able to retain its flexibility, making it akin to Sir Francis Drake's small, maneuverable and fast ships, which ultimately brought victory for the English over the bulky ships of the Spanish Armada in 1588.

Now, just four centuries later, the small, mobile educational alternatives like Philadelphia's Parkway Program offer our children a chance to attain a new American academic victory over ignorance, a victory where the absence of coercion can make room for a new morality and a system of ethics to foster more humane relations in a society that is fast becoming polarized instead of united.

Jonathan Kozol, the Pulitzer Prize-winning author of *Death at an Early Age,* has recently pinpointed the reasons for the breakdown of our presently constituted public educational enterprise. In a cogent article entitled "Look, This System is Not Working!" in *The New York Times,* April 1, 1971, he charged:

> . . . schools do not exist to free their clients from the agencies of mass persuasion. School and media possess a productive monopoly upon the imagination of the child.
>
> It is not bizarre, it is not unexpected, it is entirely logical, that public schools should serve the public interest in this fashion. That we can continually lose sight of the indoctrinational function of the public school is only perhaps the more persuasive evidence that we ourselves are well indoctrinated.
>
> Indoctrinational schooling and the mandatory practice of a twelve-year house arrest are the keystone of a mighty archway in this nation. It will not be taken out without grave consequences for the structure it supports; nor will it be taken away without the kind of struggle and the kind of sacrifice for which young people in this nation are now only beginning to prepare themselves.[7]

How do the Parkway Program, the West Philadelphia Community Free Schools, and the other Free Schools across the country fit into this dark portrait painted by Kozol? The very nature of these innovative institutions makes their primary mission a subversive and incompatible one in the eyes of the public school admin-

[7] *The New York Times,* April 1, 1971, p. 41.

istrators who are pledged to maintain the status quo. These archaic, inept, and unattractive institutions are "not suicidal," according to Kozol, so they will not take to these new challenges lightly.

As a liberating force, the Parkway Program is one of the few frontier experiments that is actually working within the system, because it encourages the students to use their acquired information to produce meaningful leverage *on* the society around them and not just docilely to sop up and store information *about* the system until after they graduate.

To accomplish this goal, the leaders of experimental educational projects like the Parkway Program and the Free Schools now sprouting up all over the country need to keep their "cool" and not let their egos get the best of them in what they are trying to do. Cliff Brenner believes that one of the great failings of our present educational system and the attempts to reform it is the intellectual arrogance shown by so many educators who feel that their ideas are the *only* ones that can save mankind.

"This attitude inhibits educational change," he observed. "What we really need is a plurality of approaches to solve our educational problems and not just concentrate on a school-without-walls approach exclusively. I feel we are now on the verge of discovering them."

Back in the late sixties, Brenner called an associate into the Philadelphia School Board president's office, where he had a desk. He pointed out the window and asked his visitor, "What do you see out there?"

"A 1965 Dodge," his perplexed friend answered.

"No," said Brenner quietly. "You see the Parkway—with its Art Museum, Library, Franklin Institute, Rodin Museum, Academy of Sciences, and all the other cultural buildings. Why can't we use these facilities in place of building a new $15 million high school?"

His vision ultimately became a reality, and now after the Parkway Program has become operational, his initial concept has more than proved its practicability. Not only did Brenner help to save the city and a nearly bankrupt school system over $15 million in capital outlay, but more importantly, he helped to place Philadelphia in the forefront as a pioneer educational metropolis in the transition stage to a new type of school system.

Art students of the Parkway Program sketching in the Philadelphia Art Museum.

Philadelphia has been one city that has been willing to gamble the lives of some of its children on a series of educational reform ideas—of which the Parkway Program has been the crown jewel —in an effort to help a decaying city to regain its once robust health and rekindle its lost soul. The hope of America is that other cities might pick up the torch and follow the lead of the City of Brotherly Love in a new Spirit of '76 that will finally give us—in the words of John Bremer, "an educational system truly worthy of itself."

Epilogue

"Tomorrow's school will be a school without walls—a school built of doors which open to the entire community.

"Tomorrow's school will reach out to the places that enrich the human spirit—to the museums, the theatres, the art galleries, to the parks and rivers and mountains.

"It will ally itself with the city, its busy streets and factories, its assembly lines and laboratories—so that the world of work does not seem an alien place for the student."

President Lyndon Baines Johnson, from a speech delivered before the American Association of School Administrators, February, 1967—some nine months before Cliff Brenner sent his memo spelling out the details of the unborn Parkway Program through the administrative channels of the Philadelphia school system.

Initial Parkway Program
Student Schedule

TIME	MON	TUES.	WED.	THURS.	FRI.		SAT.	SUN.
8:00 am to 9:00 am	*Physical Education (?)*						FREE	FREE
9:00 am to 11:00 am	Ed. com. / F.O.	Ed. com. / F.O.	Ed. com. / F.O.	Ed. com. / F.O.	Ed. com. + Indiv. Study	STAFF mtg.		
11:00 am to 1:00 pm	Man. Gr. / Lunch	Man. Gr. / Lunch	FREE	Man. Gr. / Lunch	Man. Gr. / Lunch			
1:00 pm to 3:00 pm	Tutorial	Tutorial	FREE	Tutorial	Seminar			
3:00 pm to 5:00 pm	Ed. com. / F.O.	Ed. com. / F.O.	FREE	Ed. com. / F.O.	Ed. com. / F.O.			

KEY: Ed.com. = Educational Component (e.g., institutional offering)
F.O. = Faculty Offering
Man.Gr. = Managerial Group

[FREE] : time allotted for total group activities, individual study, whatever

[Seminar] is mandatory

180

Parkway Program Bibliography

A. *Periodicals*

National Publications

American Education Publications:
"Know Your World": May 7, 1969
"The American Teacher": Jan., 1970
Changing Education: Spring, 1969
Education Digest: Sept., 1969
Junior League Magazine: Sept.-Oct., 1969
Life: May 16, 1969
Media and Methods: Jan., 1970
Nation's Schools: Sept., 1969
Parents' Magazine: Sept., 1969
Saturday Review: May 17, 1969
Scholastic Teacher: Dec., 1969
School Management: Dec., 1969
Think (IBM): Nov./Dec., 1969
Youth: June 7, 1970

Local Publications

Annual Report of the City of Philadelphia: 1968-69
Center City Philadelphian: Apr., 1969/Feb., 1970
Delaware Valley Science and Engineering Newsletter: Nov./Dec., 1969
DRPA Log: June, 1969
New Jersey Education Association Review: Sept., 1969
Urban School Report (N.J.), Nov. 1, 1969
The Evening Bulletin, Magazine (Philadelphia), Feb. 22, 1970

Institutional Publications

Amalgamated News (Amalgamated Clothing Workers): May 2, 1969
Franklin Institute News: Summer, 1969; Fall, 1969
Smith Kline and French News: June 6, 1969

Newspapers: The following newspapers have published articles on the Parkway Program:

The *Ambler Gazette*
The *Boston Globe*
The *Christian Science Monitor*
Distant Drummer
The *London Evening News*
The *London Sun*
The *Los Angeles Times*
The *Evening Bulletin* (Philadelphia)
The *Philadelphia Daily News*
The *Philadelphia Inquirer*
The *New York Times*
The *San Francisco Chronicle*
The *Toronto Daily Star*
The *Washington Star*
The *Times* (London)
The *Wall Street Journal*
The *Kansas City Star*

Foreign Publications
Orbit (Toronto, Canada), Sept., 1969

B. *Books on Allied Educational Subjects*

Ackerman, N. *et al, Summerhill: For and Against.* New York: Hart Publishing Co., Inc., 1970.

Birmingham, John, ed., *Our Time Is Now: Notes from the High School Underground.* New York: Praeger Publishers, Inc., 1970.

Borton, Terry, *Reach, Touch and Teach.* New York: McGraw-Hill Book Company, 1970.

Bremer, John, and Von Moschzisker, Michael, *School Without Walls.* New York: Holt, Rinehart & Winston, 1971.

Clinchy, Evans, *The College in the City, an Alternative.* New York: Ford Foundation, Report of the Educational Facilities Laboratories, 1969.

Dennison, George, *The Lives of Children: The Story of the First Street School.* New York: Random House, Inc., 1970.

Fantini, Mario, and Weinstein, G., *Toward Humanistic Education.* New York: Praeger Publishers, Inc., 1969.

Gross, Beatrice and Ronald, eds., *Radical School Reform.* New York: Simon & Schuster, Inc., 1970.

Herndon, James, *The Way It Spozed to Be.* New York: Simon & Schuster, Inc., 1968.

Kohl, Herbert, *The Open Classroom: A Practical Guide to a New Way of Teaching.* New York: Random House, Inc., 1970.

National Education Association, *Schools for the 70s and Beyond: A Call for Action.* Washington, D.C.: National Education Assoc., 1971.

Neill, A. S., *Summerhill: A Radical Approach to Child Rearing.* New York: Hart Publishing Co., Inc., 1970 (rev.).

182

Postman, Neil, and Weingartner, Charles, *Teaching as a Subversive Activity.* New York: The Delacorte Press, 1969.
——————————, *The Soft Revolution, A Student Handbook for Turning Schools Around.* New York: The Delacorte Press, 1971.
Repo, Satu, ed., *This Book Is About Schools.* New York: Pantheon Books, Inc., 1971.
Resnik, Henry S., *Turning on the System: War in the Philadelphia Public Schools.* New York: Pantheon Books, Inc., 1970.
Silberman, Charles E., *Crisis in the Classroom: The Remaking of American Education.* New York: Random House, Inc., 1970.

C. *Films, Videotapes, and Tape Recordings*
The following have complete documentaries on the Program:
The Canadian Television Network
Educational Television Branch, Ontario Dept. of Education
NBC-TV
National Educational TV
New York University
U.S. Information Agency
WCAU-TV Philadelphia
WPVI-TV Philadelphia
WUHY Radio Philadelphia
KYW-TV Philadelphia

D. *Supplementary Reference List of "Open Schools"*
Union for Experimenting Colleges and Universities, *University Without Walls* (Ford Foundation and U.S. Office of Education program for 1971), Antioch College, Yellow Springs, Ohio 45387.
New Nation Seed Fund (for Free School Movement), established by George Dennison, Paul Goodman, Nat Hentoff, John Holt, and Jonathan Kozol, 1971, P.O. Box 4026, Phila., Pa.
Non-Residential College (Ford and Carnegie grant, 1971). Box 6096, Albany, N.Y. 12206.
Outside the Net (a quarterly on alternative schools), P.O. Box 184, Lansing, Michigan (incorp. Liberation News Service).

Appendix A
Finding Out About
Free Schools[1]

THE SOURCES OF information about free schools are many and varied, but tap one and it will lead to many others. Here are a few to start with:
New Schools Exchange (2840 Hidden Valley Lane, Santa Barbara, California 93103)—the best single source of information on free schools: where they are, how to start one, problems to anticipate, and almost anything else you need to know.

The Big Rock Candy Mountain (Portola Institute, Inc., 1115 Merrill Street, Menlo Park, California 94025)—a new publication similar to the popular Whole Earth Catalogue, but devoted to "resources for ecstatic education." The catalogue reviews schools, teaching methods, toys and games, publications, teaching laboratories, films, tapes, records, and highlights new approaches that "make the student himself the content of his learning," are nonmanipulative, and encourage exploration and creativity ($4 per copy; $8 per year subscription—two issues plus four supplements).

The Free Learner—a remarkably complete survey of experimental schools in the San Francisco Bay area, compiled by Constance Woulf *(4615 Canyon Road, El Sobrante, California 94803)*, available at $2 a copy.

New Schools Manual—a mimeographed booklet put out by New Directions Community School *(445 Tenth Street, Richmond, California 94801)* that provides some useful clues for meeting bureaucratic rules and regulations.

Directory of Free Schools—a list of free schools across the country, published by Alternatives Foundation *(1526 Gravenstein Highway, Sebastopol, California 97452)*. The pamphlet includes an essay on "How to Start a Free School," by Frank Lindenfield, founder of several California free schools.

A Bibliography for the Free School Movement—a wide-ranging list of books on children and education, published by the Summerhill Society *(339 Lafayette Street, New York, N.Y. 10012)*. Available for 50 cents.

[1] Reprinted from "The Rise of the 'Free School' " by Bonnie Barrett Stretch, *Saturday Review*, June 20, 1970, p. 78.

185

Appendix B
A Partial List of Cooperating
Agencies in the Parkway
Program: Philadelphia

Academy of Natural Sciences
Addressograph-Multigraph Corp.
American Civil Liberties Union
American Friends Service
  Committee
American Red Cross
Archdiocese of Philadelphia
Art Alliance
Atlantic Richfield
B. Bornstein and Sons
Catholic Youth Organization
Center City Hospital
Center City Magazine
Center for the Whole Person
City Hall
Comet Camera Repair Co.
Commission on Human Relations
Committee of Seventy
Convention and Tourist Bureau
Council for Professional Craftsmen
County Court
County Medical Association
Day Nursery for the Deaf
Delaware Valley Regional Planning
  Commission
Drama Guild
Drexel Institute of Technology
Evening and Sunday Bulletin
Fellowship Commission
Fidelity Mutual Life Insurance
  Company
Film Media Center
First Baptist Church

First Presbyterian Church
Franklin Institute
General Electric
General Tire Co.
Gratz College
Greater Philadelphia Chamber of
  Commerce
Greater Philadelphia Movement
Hahnemann Medical College and
  Hospital
Health and Welfare Council of
  Greater Philadelphia Metropolitan
  Area
Horizon House
Industrial Valley Bank Building
Insurance Company of North
  America
IBM
JCRC
John F. Kennedy Vocational Center
Joy Camp Co.
KYW
McCarrie School of Dentistry
Metropolitan Associates of
  Philadelphia
Moore College of Art
Municipal Services Building
NAACP
Neupauer Conservatory of Music
NYU Educational Network
Parochial Schools Administration
  Building
Peale House
Pearl Buck Foundation

Penn Center
Pennsylvania Academy of Fine Arts
First Pennsylvania Bank
Pennsylvania Railroad: Suburban
    Station
People for Human Rights
Philadelphia 1976 Bicentennial
    Corporation
Philadelphia Board of Education
Philadelphia College of Art
Philadelphia Community College
Philadelphia Credit Bureau
Philadelphia Daily News
Philadelphia Free Library
Philadelphia Gas Works
Philadelphia Inquirer
Philadelphia Magnet School of
    Languages
Philadelphia Museum of Art
Philadelphia Music Academy
Philadelphia National Bank
Philadelphia Tribune
Philadelphia Wireless Technical
    Institute
Philadelphia Zoo
Pocket Playhouse
Police Administration Building
Pomerantz Office Supplies
Print Club
Regional Film Library
Resistance Print Shop

Rodin Museum
Smith Kline and French
Society Hill Playhouse
Society to Protect Children
Spectrum Film Processing
Swedenborgian Church
Taurus Leather Co.
Temple University
J. Reid Thomson, Architect
Unitarian Church
United Gas Improvement
United Health Services
University of Massachusetts School
    of Education
University of Pennsylvania
Urban Coalition
Urban League
John Wanamaker Philadelphia
Weinstein Geriatrics Center
YMCA of Philadelphia
YMHA of Philadelphia
YWCA of Philadelphia
YWHA of Philadelphia
WCAU
WFIL
WIBF
WIBG
WIP Radio
WKBS
World Affairs Council
WPEN
WUHY

Index

189

190